Detective Scott Hotard is a detective with the Iberia Parish Sheriff's Office located in Iberia Parish, Louisiana. He has been involved in twenty-four homicide investigations. It is his belief that every law enforcement officer has one case that will define their career.

During his career, he has worked as a patrolman, narcotics agent, K-9 officer, crime scene investigator, evidence custodian, detective and supervisor of detectives.

Detective Hotard met Detective Russell Duplantis while working together. Det. Hotard always had a fascination with this case after watching the movie 'Dead Man Walking' and when he found out Det. Duplantis was the actual case agent, he had to hear the story. Det. Hotard always knew something about the movie 'Dead Man Walking' did not add up. Det. Hotard and Det. Duplantis would become good friends and after forty years, Det. Duplantis agreed to give his story and have Det. Hotard write this book.

This book is dedicated to the memory of David LeBlanc and Loretta Bourque, taken from this world much too soon.

Scott Hotard

HE WAS A DEAD MAN WALKING

AUSTIN MACAULEY PUBLISHERS™

LONDON • CAMBRIDGE • NEW YORK • SHARJAH

A CIP catalogue record for this title is available from the British Library.

ISBN 9781528922210 (Paperback)
ISBN 9781528963718 (ePub e-book)

www.austinmacauley.com

First Published (2020)
Austin Macauley Publishers Ltd
25 Canada Square
Canary Wharf
London
E14 5LQ

Scott Hotard would like to thank 16th Judicial District Attorney, Bo Duhe, for allowing access to the original case file for this book.

Chapter 1
The Two Manikins

Preston, Billy and Tim had just finished eating a late lunch and were walking around in the yard when Preston asked them if they wanted to go rabbit hunting. The weather was cool and partly cloudy with a slight breeze. Preston thought they would see a few rabbits today. Billy and Tim agreed and told their parents they were going hunting in the sugar cane fields behind their house.

The three boys were all young teenagers. Good boys who often helped the family in the sugar cane fields. The sugar cane was tall and green just waiting to be harvested. It would be another month before the sugar cane would be cut down, burned and then loaded into trailers and pulled by big tractors to the sugar mills.

The boys walked about a mile down the headland of the sugar cane fields and came upon a small area with oil field equipment and big rusty tanks. Right past the tanks was a shell road that went into a wooded area. There were tall trees on both sides of the road. The boys knew this area because the locals used it as a dumpsite.

The boys began to walk on the shell road into the wooded area when something on the right suddenly caught Preston's eyes. He looked to his right toward an old trash pile that consisted of old roofing shingles and asbestos siding. The grass was tall in the area so Preston walked up to see what had caught his eye. Little did they know what they were looking at would eventually scare the boys like they have never been scared before.

As Preston and the other boys walked toward the trash pile, they stopped and took a double take. They asked each other, "What is that? I wonder who threw two manikins on the trash pile." They grabbed some sticks and walked up to the manikins and started poking them. Suddenly it dawned on them, those weren't two manikins, those were two human bodies.

The boys dropped the sticks and without saying a word to each other, started running home as fast as they could run. As they ran, it seemed like they weren't going anywhere. The mile they had walked seemed like it turned into ten miles. The closer they would get to their home, the farther away it seemed to be. But they kept running and running. They were not only scared because they had never seen any dead bodies before but also scared someone might still be in the wooded area and would kill them.

Finally, the boys arrived home. They were out of breath, and it took everything they had to start yelling. Family members came running out of the houses in the area to see what the boys were yelling about. After catching his breath Preston started saying, "Bodies, bodies, dead bodies."

Mr. Harold, Preston's dad, a tall man with big strong arms from working the sugar cane fields, asked, "What are you talking about?"

Preston just kept saying, "Bodies, bodies, dead bodies." Tim finally calmed down enough to say, "There are two dead bodies in the trash pile." Mr. Harold looked at Preston and asked if that's what he's trying to say, and all Preston could do was shake his head up and down. Mr. Harold placed his hands on Preston's shoulders trying to calm him down.

"Look at me, look at me," Mr. Harold began to tell Preston. As Preston raised his head, Mr. Harold said, "Preston, you mean to tell me there are two dead bodies in the old trash pile?"

Preston said, "Yea, they back there." Mr. Harold then hollered for someone to call the sheriff's office. Harold's wife, Betty, ran into the house to make the call.

"Hello, this is the Iberia Parish Sheriff's Office. What is your emergency?" It was the Iberia Parish Sheriff's Office dispatcher, Lisa, a very talkative woman who spoke faster than a Boeing 747. Betty started stuttering as she told Lisa, "They got two dead bodies out here, send somebody quickly."

Lisa responded, "Mam, you said you have two dead bodies?"

Betty said, "Yea, send somebody now." Lisa then asked Betty to calm down and tell her where the bodies were located. Betty told Lisa, "The two bodies are in a sugar cane field behind my house. My son and his cousins found them. Send somebody please."

Lisa was finally able to get Betty to tell her the address to her home. Lisa then advised Betty she would have a deputy on his way. Lisa then hung up the phone and called Chief Jim Desormeaux telling him what Betty had reported. Chief Desormeaux: a man who always said what was on his mind and not thinking about anyone else's feelings when he said it, told Lisa to send a deputy to the scene, contact the detectives, and he would also be on his way.

As she hung up the phone, Lisa called out on the radio for Deputy Pat Dominque. Pat replied, and Lisa advised him to go to Betty's home located on Old Jeanerette Rd. Betty Richards reported her boy finding two dead bodies in the sugar cane field. Deputy Dominque advised Lisa he was going pick up Deputy Joe Menard and would be on his way to Betty's house. Deputy Dominque had been working with the department for a few years. Deputy Menard was kinda blue under the collar. He was still learning the ropes.

Lisa, who was nervous, stopped to gain her composure. She then picked up the telephone to start calling to notify Det. Capt. Horace Comeaux and Det. Lt. Russell Duplantis. Lisa called Capt. Comeaux at his residence and told him about the two bodies and that he needed to head to the crime scene.

Lisa then started to call Lt. Duplantis. Lt. Duplantis was a quiet man who always seemed to be deep in thought. He was well-known and liked by everyone he met. Lisa began to dial his number when she stopped. She remembered Lt. Duplantis was spending the day with his wife. They were celebrating his wife's birthday. Lisa dreaded calling Lt. Duplantis and ruining his night, but she had to make the call. Looking down on her desk she saw the phone number to the Essanee Theater. Lt. Duplantis had called in earlier advising her he was taking his wife to see *Star Wars*.

The phone was ringing and was answered by Cindy who works in the ticket booth at the Essanee Theater. Any time one of the detectives went to watch a movie there, policy was, they would check in with Cindy and let her know where they would be sitting in case the department called for them. When Cindy answered the phone, Lisa asked her if Lt. Duplantis was there watching the movie. Cindy advised, yes Lt. Duplantis had checked in with her and was getting ready to watch *Star Wars*. The movie hadn't started yet. Lisa then asked Cindy to have Lt. Duplantis call the sheriff's office dispatcher as soon as possible.

Cindy hung up the phone, grabbed her flashlight, and walked into the theater's auditorium. She shined the light where Lt. Duplantis said he would be sitting, saw and waved for him to follow her. Lt. Duplantis exited his chair and walked to the front lobby area. Cindy then told him the department dispatcher called for him.

The dispatcher had to call for Lt. Duplantis by landline telephone because back in 1977 there were no pagers or cell phones. Once he received the message to call the dispatcher, Lt. Duplantis advised his wife Violet, the dispatcher called, and they needed to go to the sheriff's office. The office was only two blocks away. Once they arrived at the sheriff's office, Lisa informed him about the two bodies. Lt. Duplantis drove his wife home and headed to the crime scene. Little did Det. Duplantis know, but now, even after 40 years, he has never watched the movie *Star Wars*. This case would take a hold of him like no other case before and no other case after this one. He would learn to run away from anything that would bring back memories of this case. This is the case that would define a long and distinguished law enforcement career.

It was about 3:30 p.m. when Deputies Dominque and Menard arrived at Betty's house. Mr. Harold walked over to the deputies and told them his son Preston and his two cousins went rabbit hunting in the sugar cane field and found two dead bodies in the old trash dump. Deputy Dominque asked if that was the old dump by the oil field tanks, and Mr. Harold said, "Yes." Deputies Dominque and Menard then had the three boys get in their patrol car and drove out to the trash pile. Mr. Harold and Betty followed behind them in their truck.

When they arrived at the trash pile, the boys got out and pointed, saying over there and ran back to Mr. Harold's truck. Mr. Harold and Betty got out of the truck and watched as the deputies walked on the little shell road into the wooded area with their guns drawn. They didn't want to walk into the woods and not be prepared because the suspect could still be there.

Deputy Dominque walked up to the trash pile on the right and couldn't believe his eyes. There were two bodies lying face down on top of the trash pile. He couldn't tell if it was boys' or girls'. Deputy Dominque then advised Deputy Menard to go to the patrol car and call in on the radio, he had located the bodies and have the detectives called out.

As Deputy Menard walked back to the car, Chief Desormeaux was walking up to the scene. Deputy Menard told Chief Desormeaux, "There are two dead bodies, but we don't know if they are boys or girls." He then walked to the car and called dispatch on the radio to send out the detectives and the Iberia Parish Coroner Dr. Joseph Musso.

Sheriff Gerald Wattingny arrived on scene. Sheriff Wattingny was a straightforward man, very kind man, but also a firm man who was very hands on with running his department. If anything happened in his parish, he wanted to know. If it was some type of an emergency, he would always go to the scene. Chief Desormeaux had called him about the bodies and the sheriff, being who he was, headed straight to the scene.

Sheriff Wattingny walked over and looked at the bodies and turned to Chief Desormeaux and said, "If it's the last thing

I do, I will catch the people who did this. Those poor kids didn't deserve to die." Sheriff Wattingny took a closer look when Deputy Desormeaux told him the two kids had been executed. Both shot in the back of the head. Sheriff Wattingny's heart sank into his chest.

Lt. Duplantis and Capt. Comeaux both arrived to the scene about the same time. They always work homicide cases together. Other department employees would help with the cases, but in the end, it was always their responsibility to investigate and solve these cases. This was the beginning of a long, hard, case that would eventually change their lives forever.

Chapter 2
I Am Lt. Russell Duplantis

Det. Lt. Russell Duplantis was raised in a little community called the Town of Delcambre, La., which is located 8 miles west of New Iberia, La. Delcambre is a quiet little town, and everyone seems to know each other. The Police Department has a chief, one officer for the day shift, one officer for the night shift, and one dispatcher during the day. After hours calls for Delcambre are dispatched by the Iberia Parish Sheriff's Office. If something major happened in Delcambre on the east side of town, they would call the Iberia Parish Sheriff's Office for assistance, and if anything happened on the west side of town, they would call for assistance from the Vermillion Parish Sheriff's Office. It just so happens that the parish line runs through the middle of town.

Det. Duplantis attended Delcambre High School. While in school he ran track, played football and baseball. After high school he immediately joined the military. He was Army Infantry 4th Division. After serving four years in the army he returned to the Town of Delcambre. Russell as he was known at the time, married a young woman from Loreauville, La. and started working in the oilfield and at the salt mine. In 1970, he went to work for the Iberia Parish Sheriff's Office as a dispatcher. He would eventually be promoted to patrol, patrol sergeant, patrol lieutenant and lieutenant of detectives. He would eventually divorce his first wife, whom I will call Margaret and later marry his second wife, Violet. He describes Violet as the love of his life, and they have now been married for over 42 years.

Russell explained that being in law enforcement, the job becomes a part of you just as your wife is a part of you. You have to always work to keep your marriage working the same, and you have to always work to keep your mind in the game with this job. Because of this, Russell and Margaret divorced. She was not from a law enforcement family and thus, did not understand what it took to be a detective. How the work would keep you away from home and almost seem like you were married to your job instead of your wife.

The reason I decided not to mention names of some people involved in this case is because this case, which was eventually solved, was so close to home for Russell and his family, that it's almost scary. Never in his wildest dreams did he think he would face what was about to become a reality for him when he started investigating this case.

When Lt. Duplantis started working in detectives, he worked alongside Capt. Horace Comeaux. Capt. Comeaux was a veteran of World War II who, just as Lt. Duplantis, became married to the job. Lt. Duplantis and Capt. Comeaux investigated all of the homicides and suicides in the Parish of Iberia. Because the department was small, they would also work thefts, burglaries and rapes, but ultimately, they were responsible for investigating the homicides. Back then, there were about four to five homicides per year. They were the detectives assigned to work this case. Because this case became so big there were several other officers involved in the investigation as well as the St. Martin Parish Sheriff's Office.

Lt. Russell Duplantis said if anyone ever worked as a detective in law enforcement, they would surely have a case that defined their career. The one case that kept you up at night. The one case that haunted you. The one case you could never put out of your mind and couldn't go home and talk to your wife about. Even after 40 years, Lt. Duplantis was still haunted by the case this book is written about. The way he explained it is, he departmentalized it in his mind. It is something that a person wants to forget but can't. The only people you can talk to about these types of cases are other law enforcement officers. They understand what you go through whereas family and friends would just not understand. Not to mention if he had told someone about the case and they went around talking about it, there would surely be repercussions. Not in the sense that he would get in trouble but in the sense that it could ruin the entire investigation and possibly help the suspects walk free.

A lot of man-hours were put into solving this case. It became a part of who you were. A part of your life that is there to stay, no matter how hard you try to forget it.

While being interviewed for this book Lt. Duplantis said he actually has two cases that define his career. This case and another case involving a five-year-old girl. He tells the story of a wife whose husband worked offshore and would be gone for several days at a time. On one occasion, while her husband was offshore, she had another man come stay with her, her two boys and daughter at their home. The little girl who I will call Susan confronted her mom who I will call Janice, about her having another man in the house. Susan told Janice, she was going to tell her dad that Janice had another man staying in the house with them when he came in from offshore. Janice panicked and had to come up with a plan to keep her husband from finding out about the other man.

Janice did come up with a plan. She drove to the school, Center Street Elementary, located on Center St. in New Iberia, La. pretending to drop Susan off at school. Susan was in Pre-K or Kindergarten. Instead of dropping Susan off at school, Janice then drove her to a sugar cane field. Because it was close to Christmas time, the sugarcane was very tall. If someone drove into the sugar cane field, no one would be able to see you.

Once driving into the sugar cane field, Janice told Susan to get out of the car and go stand on the headland of the sugar cane field. Not knowing what her mother was about to do, Susan obeyed and got out and stood in front of the car. Before Susan had a chance to react to what was happening, Janice put the car into gear, pressed the gas pedal and ran over her own child. Janice got out of the car to see if Susan was still alive because she saw her, Susan's little body shaking. Thinking she had to finish the job, Janice broke the rear-view mirror of the windshield and started hitting Susan's little head until there was blood everywhere. Janice drove home and later called to report Susan didn't come home from school and was missing.

What struck Lt. Duplantis the most about this case was two-fold. First, how can a mother do something like this to her own child? Second, after she served her time in prison, the husband took her back.

Lt. Duplantis would eventually leave the Iberia Parish Sheriff's Office. Sheriff Wattingny lost the election to newly elected Sheriff Romo Romero who took office on July 1, 1980. Sheriff Wattingny, after 24 years as sheriff, left the department and went into private business starting his own security business which was called 3 Division Security. The company provided security services, investigations, guard services and alarm systems. Lt. Duplantis and Capt. Comeaux both went to work for 3 Division. After three or four years, Sheriff Wattingny sold the business so Lt. Duplantis took his family and moved to Palm Beach Florida. He would work at the police department there for the next 17 years. The same as with the Iberia Parish Sheriff's Office, Lt. Duplantis worked patrol, was promoted to patrol sergeant and for the last two years he worked for internal affairs.

Lt. Duplantis retired from the Palm Beach Police Department and moved to Georgia. He and his wife Violet had built a little cabin in the Blue Ridge Mountains. Not long after, Lt. Duplantis' mother and his mother-in-law both were diagnosed with cancer so he and Violet decided it was time to move back to Louisiana because their family needed them. Lt. Duplantis returned to New Iberia and went to work for Sheriff Sidney Hebert at the Iberia Parish Work Release Center. The work release center was part of the jail, but the inmates there were provided jobs. They would be taken to work each day and picked up from work and brought back to the work release center every evening.

On July 1, 2008, the newly elected Sheriff Louis Ackal took office. He asked Lt. Duplantis to stay on and work for him as a detective in the sex offender division. To this day Lt. Duplantis is working for the Iberia Parish Sheriff's Office. The department is where I, Det. Scott Hotard met Lt. Duplantis and is also where we decided it was time for this story to be told. The detective side of the story for *Dead Man Walking*. A nun by the name of Sister Helen Prejean wrote a book about her story in *Dead Man Walking,* and the Bourque family wrote about their story in *Dead Family Walking.* Now we have this book, *He Was a Dead Man Walking.* After 40 years, Lt. Duplantis is now telling his story.

Chapter 3
Two Class Rings

It was dark by the time Lt. Duplantis and Capt. Comeaux arrived at the scene. When they arrived, Assistant District Attorney, Dracos Burke and the D.A.'s investigator Dean Burley were just leaving the scene.

Mr. Burley had taken photos of the crime scene, and Mr. Burke wanted to see the scene because if the case was ever solved, he would be the Assistant D.A. who would prosecute the case. Major Sonny Tyler also arrived on scene and would later play a role in the investigation.

Mr. Burke worked as a military lawyer in the United States Navy (JAG Officer) before going to work for the 16th Judicial District Attorney's Office. He was known as a meticulous prosecutor who covered every little detail. From stories told, he never lost a case. Little did Mr. Burke know at the time, but this case, would be the biggest case of his career. He would argue this case all the way to the United States Supreme Court. And yes, he won.

Lt. Duplantis and Capt. Comeaux approached the trash pile to view the bodies. Lt. Duplantis told Capt. Comeaux it looked like the kids were holding hands when they died. Capt. Comeaux agreed.

Parish Coroner Dr. Joseph Musso was already on scene and declared the teenage boy and teenage girl deceased. He had the bodies removed by Acadian Ambulance and taken to Iberia General Hospital. The Iberia Parish Morgue was located at the hospital. The bodies were still clothed, and it did not appear anything had been taken from them. This told detectives the murders were not the result of a robbery gone bad.

There was something both kids were wearing when they were murdered, and little did anyone know that those items would be how officers were able to get some sort of identification. The items worn by the victims were their graduation rings. Both rings had their initials on them. The girl's ring had the initials LB, and the school was New Iberia Senior High School class of 1977. The boy's ring had the initials DL, and the school was Catholic High School class of 1978.

Chief Jim Desormeaux had the Iberia Parish Dispatcher contact officials from both schools to see if they could help identify the two teens by using their class rings. School officials from New Iberia Senior High identified the female ring as possibly belonging to Loretta Bourque. School officials from Catholic High School identified the male class ring as possibly belonging to David LeBlanc. The school officials from both schools provided Chief Desormeaux with addresses and phone numbers for the families of Loretta and David.

Chief Desormeaux was never one to sugar coat anything. He did not know how to show compassion, or, he might not have wanted too. He was known as a rough character in life and in his mannerism. No one really knows, but it was thought at the time, that Chief Desormeaux didn't realize the hurt and pain he was about to cause for the victim's families. Instead of sending someone to the homes and talk to the parents, he called them by phone.

Can you imagine being told over the phone that your son or daughter was found dead with three bullet holes in the back of the head? Would you as a parent become so confused and upset that you wouldn't know what to do? Do you think you would have been able to go to the morgue and identify your child? That's exactly what David and Loretta's parents had to do.

Family members later arrived at the morgue and positively identified the bodies as Loretta Bourque and David

LeBlanc. Now that the bodies had been identified, the case started to take shape. Dr. Joseph Musso would perform the autopsies that same night.

Detectives learned from the parents that both kids had gone out the night before to attend the Catholic High School Homecoming football game and never returned home. The kids were reported missing, and David's car had been found on a headland located off Seiber Rd. in St. Martin Parish earlier in the day by St. Martin Parish Sheriff's Office.

David had borrowed his sister's white Plymouth Sedan to take Loretta to the football game the previous night. Lt. Duplantis would find out much later the car is the reason David and Loretta were both killed.

The autopsies showed David and Loretta both died from three gunshots to the back of the head, execution style. Dean Burley, the investigator for the District Attorney's Office, took photos of the autopsies for evidence.

Lt. Duplantis and Capt. Comeaux began surveying the scene and attempting to locate evidence. Being experienced in investigating homicides, they noticed little things the other officers did not notice. They located shoe prints, which led to a small area of grass inside the wooded area. In the wooded area, they located a white sweater that would later be identified as belonging to Loretta.

The grassy area inside the wood-line meant there were two separate scenes. One was the scene where the bodies were located on top the trash pile, and the other scene was inside the wooded area, to the northwest side of the trash pile. It would later be discovered the grassy area is where the both suspects raped Loretta while David was handcuffed to a tree near the trash pile.

Because of darkness and it being in the year 1977, equipment wasn't available to work the crime scene at night. Proper power and lighting was not available. It was decided that a patrol deputy would stay on the scene all night and the detectives would go home and be back on scene for 8:30 a.m. A meeting was scheduled to discuss the case at 8:00 a.m. at the courthouse before going back to the scene.

During the meeting, all involved in the case told each other of their findings during the investigation so each officer would know what was known from the investigation so far and where it was going.

After the meeting, Lt. Duplantis picked up some plaster to make plaster cast of shoe prints located behind where the bodies were found. They would also find two bullets. Dr. Musso, after performing the autopsies, informed them with the direction of travel and the exit wounds, there would be at least one bullet, maybe two underneath the area where Loretta's body was found. The bullets were taken to the State Police Crime Lab in Baton Rouge for ballistics test.

Chapter 4
You're Trespassing

The day was November 4, 1977. David awoke early and headed off to school. Loretta having already graduated from high school, stayed home with her mother. David and Loretta were really looking forward to the Catholic High School Homecoming football game later in the evening.

Lt. Duplantis to this day is unsure if David and Loretta ever actually attended the homecoming game. But what he is sure about is what happened to Loretta and David the rest of that night.

Elmo Patrick Sonnier was off work and wanted to go rabbit hunting with his brother Eddie James Sonnier. It was something they did often. They were really poachers. They hunted at night using spotlights and flashlights to blind rabbits so they could shoot them. At least that's what Elmo told his wife each night before he left.

When Elmo and Eddie said they were going rabbit hunting, they would hunt rabbits, but if an opportunity was in front of them, they would take advantage of it. To them opportunity was catching young couples parking at night. When I say parking, I mean making out or having sex. To Elmo and Eddie, catching couples was their way of getting themselves off.

Elmo Patrick Sonnier was a tall man, dark brown wavy hair, long sideburns, and most of his teeth missing. Some say he wasn't the brightest tool in the shed but he was street smart. Elmo had served time in the Louisiana State Penitentiary and always vowed he would never go back.

Eddie James Sonnier was more of a quiet person and kept to himself. Well, he kept to himself when he wasn't around his brother Elmo. He was a slow learner and never really amounted to anything. Eddie was intimidated by Elmo, and when Elmo told him to do something, he did it. It didn't matter what it was, he would do it.

Elmo, his wife, kids, Eddie and their mother lived in a house on Jefferson Island Rd. in Iberia Parish. The house was old and faded white in color with an old barn nearby. The barn was falling down, but it served a purpose for Elmo and Eddie. No one knew what Elmo and Eddie used to do in that barn. Well, no one except for their victims.

During Lt. Duplantis' investigation, he found out that Elmo and Eddie were serial rapist. They would catch young couples parking, kidnap them, drive to another location and rape the girls. The boys were handcuffed to a tree and forced to watch. Through his investigation Lt. Duplantis estimated that Elmo and Eddie did this to at least 25 to 30 couples.

Elmo and Eddie, when caught, would both admit to the many rapes. In fact, they couldn't remember how many couples but would know they had been doing this for over a year. The barn next to their house is one of the many locations they would take the couples. They would handcuff the boy to the barn, place a blanket in a stall on the ground, and there, would rape the girls.

Another location they would kidnap young couples and rape girls is the keystone locks located on Hwy 31 between New Iberia and St. Martinville and a location near Jefferson Island off the Jefferson Island Rd.

Elmo and Eddie headed out to go hunting. They had driven around in Elmo's old, blue Dodge Dart for a while and did not see any rabbits, so they decided to try Seiber Rd. They were hunting off a headland with flashlights and .22 caliber rifles. It was strange, but Elmo always wore gloves while rabbit hunting.

After the football game, David and Loretta were back in St. Martinville at about 9:30 p.m. when they saw Theresa driving on Main St. Theresa and Loretta were best friends and were always together when Loretta wasn't spending time with David. According to Theresa, David and Loretta were supposed to meet her at the Track Lounge at 10:00 p.m.

David saw Theresa, so he followed her to the Track Lounge. The Track Lounge is where all the young people hung out. Back then, a person 18 years old could go into a bar and drink alcohol. When they drove up in the parking lot, David stayed in the car while Loretta got out and talked to Theresa. Because it was a Friday night, the parking lot was full of cars and teenagers standing near their cars talking.

Loretta told Theresa they weren't going into the club because David was tired from a long day. When David and Loretta drove off, Theresa didn't know at the time, but she would never talk to her best friend ever again; it was the last time she would ever see Loretta alive.

David and Loretta left the Track Lounge and went to Seiber Rd., which was known as Lover's Lane. David drove down a shell road just around a curve so his car could not be seen from the roadway. The area had some old oil tanks and areas where the grass wouldn't grow. There were trees on the right side of the road but none on the left.

Elmo and Eddie didn't see any rabbits while hunting so they walked back toward Elmo's blue Dodge Dart. When they got closer to the car, they noticed a white four-door car parked nearby. This was another chance to catch another couple parking, and they surely wouldn't let the opportunity pass them by.

The Sonnier brothers approached David's car. Elmo shined his flashlight into David's car, startling David and Loretta who were in the back seat. Elmo, who was wearing a security company shirt, flashed a badge telling the young lovers he was a police officer and they were trespassing. Elmo made Loretta and David get out of the car. Elmo wondered why they had climbed over the seat and exit the car from the front door.

Elmo asked David and Loretta for their driver license. He told them he needed to identify them so he could call the property owner and see if they wanted to file charges for

26

trespassing. David and Loretta didn't know that Elmo was actually getting their names and addresses in case he ever had to go and look them up. He would always get the names and addresses of his victims and let them know if they ever told anyone what happened, he knew where they lived and would kill their families.

Who carries a set of handcuffs with them while hunting rabbits? Law enforcement officers don't do this. Elmo always kept his handcuffs with him because he didn't know when the next opportunity would arise. He pulled the handcuffs out and had Eddie handcuff Loretta and David together and make them get back into David's car and climb over the seat and get in the back.

Elmo noticed the back doors to the car did not have any handles. He asked David why the back doors didn't have any door handles, and David told Elmo his dad worked for the sheriff and that he got the car from a sheriff's auction. It was an old patrol car. Little did David know, but right then and there, what he had just told Elmo, signed his and Loretta's death warrants. Elmo, years later while on death row, would tell Lt. Duplantis as soon as David said his dad worked for the sheriff, Elmo knew he would have to kill them.

Once everyone was in the car, Elmo started driving down the shell road back toward Seiber Rd. From there, they drove around for a short time and eventually went to the Tastee Freeze in St. Martinville.

A young lady by the name of Gloria was working as a carhop that night at the Tastee Freeze. She walked out to the white Plymouth sedan and saw two older white males sitting in the front and David and Loretta in the back seat. She thought it was kinda strange because David and Loretta were not talking and seemed like they were scared.

Elmo and Eddie ordered two hotdogs and two shakes. Gloria brought them their order, Elmo paid for it, and they drove off. That night Gloria did not report what she had seen.

Chapter 5
Crochet Rd

Elmo told Eddie he knew of a good place they could take the young couple and decided he would drive there. Elmo, after driving for about 45 minutes, turned onto Crochet Rd. which in 1977 was still a shell road. He then turned left onto a headland on side of a sugar cane field and kept driving until he came upon some old oil field tanks and a little wooded area. Once there, he stopped the car and made Loretta and David crawl over the back seat and get out of the car. Now was the time Elmo had been waiting for. He was going to have his fun.

Elmo and Eddie walked near the back of the car for a moment and then returned. Elmo grabbed Loretta by the arm telling her he wanted to talk to her and led her into the woods. Eddie was by the car with David who was cuffed to a tree.

Elmo would ask Loretta if she wanted to go home safe, to which she replied yes. Elmo then told her he was going to have sex with her and if she complied, she and David would be going home later. Loretta was so scared that she would do anything to save David and herself from harm. Loretta was then raped without struggle.

Eddie was getting impatient. He was waiting for his turn with Loretta. It was how he and Elmo always did it. Elmo would rape the girl, and soon after Eddie always took his turn. Eddie walked into the woods wondering what was taking Elmo and Loretta so long. When Eddie found them, they were putting their clothes on. Elmo walked back to the car where David was located leaving Loretta alone with Eddie.

Eddie asked Loretta since she had sex with Elmo would she have sex with him. Loretta replied, "I will if you promise to let me and David go home safe tonight."

Eddie said, "Sure, no one is going to hurt you." Eddie then had intercourse with Loretta. They put their clothes back on and walked to the car where Elmo and David were waiting.

Loretta walked up to David and told him what she had done. She told him she gave herself because they promised if she did, they would let her and David go home safe. Even with the ordeal she had to go through, she was more worried about David and would do anything to save his life.

David's face turned red as the anger was building up inside of him. David knew if he tried to run or tried to fight, they would kill Loretta. He was not leaving her alone, and he was not going to risk Loretta's life by fighting with them. Because of his love for Loretta, he did everything they told him to do.

Just imagine for a moment. A 16-year-old boy could have saved his own life by running away. He chose to stay with Loretta. He was not leaving her all alone with Elmo and Eddie. David wanted to do something, but he knew if he tried anything, Elmo and Eddie would surely kill Loretta.

Loretta asked them if they could go home now. Eddie asked her how she and David intended on getting back to town, and she told them they would walk. Elmo and Eddie walked to the back of the car and talked about what they were going to do. What Elmo came up with was not what Eddie wanted to hear.

Elmo told Eddie they had to kill David and Loretta because David's dad was a deputy with the sheriff's office. Little did they know David's dad did work for Sheriff Fusellier of the St. Martin Parish Sheriff's Office, but he worked as a mechanic for a construction company owned by the sheriff and his brother. David's dad did not work for the sheriff's office, and he was not a deputy.

Eddie was not sure he wanted to kill anyone, but he always did what Elmo told him to do. Elmo told Eddie to make David and Loretta lay down on a trash pile. David laid down on the left, and Loretta laid down on the right. They were both face down. Elmo instructed them not to look up saying they were going to leave and once they were gone, David and Loretta would be free to go.

Elmo and Eddie were standing about four to five feet behind David and Loretta as they lay face down on the trash pile. Elmo handed Eddie a .22 caliber rifle and told him to shoot Loretta. While this was happening, David had reached over and held Loretta's hand trying to comfort her.

Eddie pointed his rifle at Loretta's head and pulled the trigger. The sound of the bullet went off. Eddie had missed his target. He was aiming for the back of Loretta's head and missed. No one will ever know if Eddie missed the shot on purpose.

Elmo grabbed the gun from Eddie and said he would do it. He then fired 1 round into the back of Loretta's head and the next round into the back of David's head. To make sure they were dead, he fired two more rounds into the back of their heads.

Elmo and Eddie left the bodies there, got into David's car, and drove back to Seiber Road. The drive was 21 miles from the location on Crochet Rd. Once they arrived, they noticed Elmo's car was sitting on a flat tire. Elmo had a small jack in his car and didn't feel like fighting with it so he decided to see what kind of jack was in David's car. He opened the trunk and found a larger jack. He used David's jack to change the tire on his car and put the jack in the trunk of his car so he could give it to his wife. She didn't have a jack for her car.

Elmo and Eddie, knowing they had committed the ultimate crime, drove toward the city of Delcambre on Jefferson Island Rd. even passing their home on the way. They came upon a location on Jefferson Island Rd. right near Jefferon Island. Elmo wrapped the two rifles in green plastic and buried them in the ground. Elmo had wrapped the guns because he had always planned on going back and getting them. Years later Lt. Duplantis asked Elmo why did he bury the guns, and Elmo's reply was as soon as the heat died down, he was going to get the guns and do it again.

They finally got home at about 4:30 a.m., and Elmo went straight to sleep. Eddie tossed and turned and could not sleep.

Chapter 6
I Saw a White Car

On November 5, 1977, at approximately 10:00 a.m., Alonzo went rabbit hunting on a shell road located off of Seiber Rd. Alonzo was a young, black male who had lived in the area all his life. He drove down the shell road as he had always done. This was a good hunting area for him because of the wooded areas at the end of the shell road. As Alonzo made the left-hand curve on the shell road, he noticed a white Plymouth sedan parked on the side of the road next to the tree line. As he drove by, he noticed the car windows were down and no one in the car.

Alonzo went hunting and returned to his car about 11:30 a.m. No luck killing rabbits that morning. While walking back, he kept wondering if the white car was still on side of the shell road. He started his car, and as he drove toward Seiber Rd., he again saw the white car. This time, not sure why someone left their car out there, Alonzo decided to look inside the car. When he took a peek inside, he saw a purse and other items on the floorboard.

Alonzo went back to his car and drove straight to the St. Martin Parish Sheriff's Office to report the car. He then showed deputies the location of the car.

Deputies were surprised to see the car. It was actually the same car they were on the lookout for. Earlier in the morning David's parents had reported, David and the car didn't return home last night. Loretta being from New Iberia, her parents had reported Loretta didn't make it home last night.

The white car was David's car (actually his sister's car). With the location of the car, the windows down and a purse on the floor. They also located the two hot dog wrappers and cups from the milkshakes inside the car. It soon became apparent there was foul play involved.

If you remember, earlier I mentioned David's father worked for Sheriff Fuselier. The sheriff was a very big man who cared for his employees, both with the sheriff's office and with his construction company. He knew the white car because he had helped David's father buy the car at the sheriff's auction.

Sheriff Fuselier had his detectives called out to the scene of the car. Capt. Bonvillain would soon arrive on scene. A mass search was set up with helicopters searching by air and deputies searching the areas by land.

A BOLO was put out by St. Marin Parish Sheriff's Office for all local departments to be on the lookout for David and Loretta and possible foul play. While the search was taking place, the bodies were found by the three kids off Crochet Rd. in Iberia Parish. It was not known at the time that the bodies were of David and Loretta. The parents found out a few hours later when they received the dreaded phone call from Chief Jim Desormeaux to go the Iberia Parish Morgue and identify the bodies.

The case had now become a kidnapping in St. Martin Parish and double homicide in Iberia Parish. The victims of the kidnapping were also the murder victims, David and Loretta.

The St. Martin Parish Sheriff's Office was now involved with a joint investigation with the Iberia Parish Sheriff's Office. On November 7, 1977, a meeting was held between the Iberia Parish Sheriff's Office and the St. Martin Parish Sheriff's Office. During the meeting Sheriff Fuselier told Lt. Duplantis and Capt. Comeaux they have carte blanche; from this point on they were now deputized in St. Martin Parish and could do whatever they had to do for their investigation.

Chapter 7
Rapes Reported

Lt. Duplantis and Capt. Comeaux spent many hours working to solve this case. Now that they knew where the crime first started, they decided to set up a stakeout operation on the shell road off of Seiber Rd.

Lt. Duplantis procured an older model car, and he began to put a plan in motion. He would drive the car out to the shell road and sit in the car along with Det. Steve Davis. Det. Davis would wear a wig and pretend to be a female parking with Lt. Duplantis. Capt. Comeuax, Major Sonny Tyler, Det. Ray Boudreaux, and Deputy Gaylord Musemeche would be hiding nearby in two other vehicles. The plan was: if a car drove down the shell road, they would wait to see if someone would get out and approach the car Lt. Duplantis and Det. Davis were in. Once the person approached the car, the other officers who were waiting in the other two cars would approach and take the suspect down.

When the plan was put together, all the officers involved were warned how dangerous the operation would be. It was decided by everyone involved that if the suspect had a gun, they would do what needed to be done. No one was going to get hurt or even killed by a psychopathic maniac who liked to kill kids.

Lt. Duplantis and Det. Davis sat in the car waiting for approximately two hours. It was to the point that they figured no one would show up. A short time later, a call came out over the radio from Capt. Comeaux. He reported seeing headlights of a car near the entrance of the shell road off of Seiber Rd. As he watched the car, it drove up slowly, came to a stop, sat for about two minutes, then drove away really fast. Capt. Comeaux and Major Tyler attempted to catch up to the car, but by the time they made it to Seiber Rd., it was gone.

Capt. Comeaux was unable to get a description of the car or the driver. Everyone felt it had to be the suspect. Years later, Elmo would tell Lt. Duplantis it was him that night in the car. He would explain he had gone out looking for couples parking on the shell road off Seiber Rd. and as he slowly drove up, for some reason the hair on the back of his neck stood up. He would say he stopped the car and looked around for a few minutes, became scared of getting caught, and drove away.

A few days later, Lt. Duplantis received a call from St. Martin Parish Det. Bonvillain who reported they had people coming out of the woodworks claiming to have been out parking and kidnapped, driven to another location, the girl being raped while the boy was cuffed to a tree or another object and forced to watch the rape. The victims were all reporting there were two suspects involved.

Alice, a woman in her early 20s, came forward to report she had been raped. She told detectives she and her boyfriend John were parking in a sugar cane field one night when someone walked up with a flashlight saying he was a police officer and flashed a badge. She said he told her and John they were on private property and he needed their driver license.

Alice went on to say that after giving their driver license, the white male suspect told them he was going to contact the land owner and see if he wanted to file charges against them for trespassing. Alice and John were handcuffed together by another white male suspect and placed into the back seat of their car and driven to another location off Hwy 31. The location was near the Keystone Locks. The land had an old barn and old farm equipment everywhere. It was later learned the land belonged to the mayor of New Iberia, J. Allen Daige.

Alice was raped while John was cuffed to a piece of old farm equipment and forced to watch. The suspects told them they knew where they lived and had their driver license and if they reported the incident to anyone, they would kill their families. They were driven back to the original location, the handcuffs were taken off, and they were free to leave.

Alice was asked if she could identify the suspect in a photo line-up, and she said yes. At the time Lt. Duplantis reported they had identified a possible suspect who worked at the sugar mill in St. Martin Parish. They put together a line-up with Lt. Duplantis being one of the six people in the line-up along with the possible suspect. Lt. Duplantis was later told Alice came unglued when she saw the line-up. She had picked Lt. Duplantis out of the line-up as the suspect because he had kinda long dark hair and long dark side burns. Lt. Duplantis said that even though he was picked out in the line-up, it gave them something to go on because now they knew the suspect looked like Lt. Duplantis.

Lt. Duplantis and Capt. Comeaux continued to work the case very hard. They went to all the local bars, restaurants and cafes. Eventually they went to the Tastee Freeze located in St, Martinville. Lt. Duplantis started asking around if anyone had possibly seen the two victims the night of the murders. A girl by the name of Gloria came forward and said she had something to tell him.

Lt. Duplantis was surprised to hear what Gloria had to say. Gloria would tell Lt. Duplantis she was working as a carhop at the Tastee Freeze on the night of November 4, 1977. Around 10:30 p.m. to 11:00 p.m., a blue Dodge Dart car drove up. Gloria said she wasn't friends with David and Loretta but knew them. She went on to say there were two older guys in the front seat and David and Loretta in the back seat. David and Loretta were just sitting there looking scared not saying anything. The two older males ordered hotdogs and shakes. After getting their food they left.

Lt. Duplantis asked Gloria why she never reported this before, and she replied she was scared. The two older white males whom she didn't know by name had frequented Tastee Freeze in the past. She was worried if she spoke to the police and the two older males found out, they would know it was her who reported them and they knew where to find her.

Lt. Duplantis said, "Gloria's information wasn't exactly correct." Gloria had put David and Loretta in a blue Dodge Dart that night with the two suspects, but they were actually in David's sister's white Plymouth. Lt. Duplantis said this information set them back a bit because they were trying to find out if the white Plymouth had gone to the Tastee Freeze and she told them a blue Dodge Dart.

Gloria would remember later that Elmo and Eddie would go to the Tastee Freeze, but they were always in the blue Dodge Dart. She got the Dodge Dart mixed up with the white Plymouth.

Lt. Duplantis asked Gloria if she would be able to give a description of the suspects to a sketch artist so he can draw their facial composites. She agreed and met them at the Iberia Parish Courthouse. The sketches were drawn, and Lt. Duplantis thought they looked like two brothers Elmo Patrick Sonnier and Eddie James Sonnier. Capt. Comeaux mentioned to Lt. Duplantis the driver's facial composite looked like him. The composite of the suspect who was driving the car while at the Tastee Freeze had dark wavy hair, moustache, long sideburns, dark complexion and bad teeth. Copies of the composites were placed all over town in St. Martinville and New Iberia.

The case became very massive. The communities in Iberia Parish and St. Martin Parish were running scared knowing there was a rapist/murderer running loose. Kids were scared at school because Loretta and David had been very popular at school. It shook the foundation of the schools because we didn't know if any other kids had been kidnapped and raped and not coming forward. We knew even with this tragedy, some kids would think nothing could happen to them and they would go out and park in the streets and stay out after dark. Kids don't sense the kind of danger they could be in.

Another witness would eventually come forward. His name was Sean. He said on the night of November 4, 1977 he drove down Seiber Rd with his girlfriend. He turned onto the shell road and drove toward the back when he came upon a blue Dodge Dart. As he drove past the Dodge Dart, he noticed there was no one inside. He went to the old oil tanks, turned around and came back and drove past the Dodge Dart as he was leaving. Again he did not see anyone in the car. He reported the time was about 1:00 a.m. which would have actually been the early morning of November 5, 1977.

Lt. Duplantis was now piecing the case together. Gloria had reported a blue Dodge Dart at Tastee Freeze and now Sean reported a blue Dodge Dart with no one inside parked on the shell road off of Seiber Rd. on the same night of the murders. The same location the white Plymouth had been located.

Chapter 8
14-Year-Old Girl

Members of the Iberia Parish Sheriff's Office held a meeting each morning to update everyone of their findings for the investigation the previous day. Major Sonny Tyler would sit in on all the meetings and take notes. He would later update Sheriff Wattingny of the investigation from his notes. His notes were a daily log of everything that was taking place during the investigation.

During one of the meetings, the blue Dodge Dart was brought up. It was decided to contact the Louisiana Department of Motor Vehicles in Baton Rouge and request a list of all the Dodge Darts sold in and around St. Martin Parish and Iberia Parish in the past two years.

The paperwork from the Department of Motor Vehicles arrived, and the task of going through it was a very slow process. The stacks of paperwork were reaching the ceiling. There were no computers or fax machines back then, so everything had to be done by hand. Off duty deputies and off duty clerical personnel were brought in to help go through the paperwork.

One evening, about two weeks into the investigation, Lt. Duplantis received a phone call from Sgt. Scelfo, who was in charge of the Iberia Parish Juvenile Detective Division. Sgt. Scelfo reported he had received information from a young 14-year-old girl that she too had been raped. For this book, we will call her Missy.

Lt. Duplantis asked Sgt. Scelfo if Missy would come in and talk to them. The next day, right after school, Missy arrived at the Iberia Parish Court House and spoke to Sgt. Scelfo, Lt. Duplantis, and Capt. Comeaux.

Missy began to give her story. One night she had plans to go to the movies with her boyfriend Edward. Her father, who was very strict, allowed her to go, but she wasn't allowed to go anywhere else. That night Missy and Edward had gone to the movies at the Essanee Theater but left early. They drove around and eventually ended up on a headland in a sugar cane field to make out. While they were parked, a white guy walked up to the car shining a flashlight and waving a badge, saying he was a police officer.

When the white man told them to get out of the car, she noticed another white guy, but this one was younger. Missy said the older guy told her and Edward they were trespassing, and he had to contact the landowner to see if they wanted to file charges. Edward was then handcuffed, and Missy was blindfolded and placed into the back seat of Edward's car. The older guy was the driver of the car.

Missy said she could remember travelling on Center St. in New Iberia heading toward Delcambre. She was able to see under the blind fold and gave the following story.

The driver drove down Hwy 14 almost to Delcambre, and there was a little motel on the left. Across from the motel was a shell road with two feet tall trees lined up on both sides, all the way down the road. Toward the end of this road she saw several yellow flashing lights on the roadway. The driver turned right, and a-little-ways down she could see some oil tanks on the left side of the road. The driver turned left on the little road that passes on side of the oil tanks. They drove a-little-ways down this road, and the driver turned into the woods. It was actually a cut-out through the woods. They came upon a clearing and were forced out of the car.

Once out of the car, Edward was handcuffed to a tree. Missy was taken into the wood-line but still in view of Edward. The older guy told her to take off her clothes. She pleaded with him saying she was a virgin and she was also on her period. The guy didn't care. He pointed a rifle at her and made her take off her clothes, and he began to rape and sodomize her. Once he was done, the younger guy raped her. She said they repeatedly raped her over and over and were very rough and hurting her.

Missy found it strange because after she was repeatedly raped, the two guys were being very nice to them. She said she and Edward wanted to walk home but the two guys insisted on driving them back to where they found them in their car. They were eventually dropped off, and the two guys left. She looked at Lt. Duplantis like she was deep in thought. Then she said, "You know, they didn't even blindfold for the trip back."

Missy, feeling scared and hurt, felt she had to tell her dad what happened to her. She started telling her dad she had been kidnapped and raped thinking he would want to find who did this to his daughter and report it to the police. She was dead wrong.

Missy's father became a person she had never known before. He didn't seem mad that she had been raped but was mad because if she had been at the movies like she was supposed to be, this would never have happened. Her dad then grabbed a belt and began beating her with the belt buckle. She was bruised everywhere.

Lt. Duplantis asked Missy if she could show them where the rape took place, and she told him she knew exactly how to get there. Lt. Duplantis, Sgt. Scelfo, Capt. Comeaux and Missy all got into Lt. Duplantis' department car, and Missy had them travel down Center St, which turns into Hwy 14. They stayed on Hwy 14 until they came upon a little motel on the left side. She had him turn right on the shell road. This is the road that leads to the entrance of Jefferson Island. Lt. Duplantis knew this road well. It was only a mile outside of the City of Delcambre where he lived. He also knew the road because a few years earlier, it was his father who had planted all the little trees along both sides of the shell road.

As Lt. Duplantis reached the end of the shell road, he could see the road construction, and there were several yellow lights flashing. The road was Jefferson Island Rd. Little did

Lt. Duplantis know at the time that the suspects lived on the same road about four miles down toward New Iberia.

Lt. Duplantis turned right onto Jefferson Island Rd. and drove a-little-ways down, and Missy told him, "That's the place, turn left." They turned left on side of the oil tanks. They travelled a few hundred feet, and Missy had him turn right into the cut-out in the woods. They drove another few hundred feet, and Missy said this was where it happened.

Missy showed them where Edward was handcuffed to the tree. Looking at the tree, Lt. Duplantis could tell there had been more than one person handcuffed to it in the past. Missy then showed them where she was raped.

Missy knew since she had gone to the sheriff's office with her story, she couldn't go home. Her dad would kill her. Instead of sending her home, Sgt. Scelfo asked her if she had any relatives she could stay with. Missy told him of family in Port Arthur Texas. Arrangements were made for Missy to be taken to Port Arthur and be with her family members. As for Missy's father, he was warned not to have any contact with Missy again and if he went to Texas to get her, he would be charged for the beating he gave her. Lt. Duplantis said, from that point on, that he had never heard from Missy again.

Chapter 9
Big Break

With all the women who had come forward reporting they had been raped, Lt. Duplantis now knew he didn't just have two murderers, they were also serial rapist. If he didn't catch them real soon, another girl would be raped and another couple might be killed.

Because they knew it was a .22 rifle that was used in the murders, Lt. Duplantis and Capt. Comeaux contacted the ATF (Alcohol Tobacco and Firearms) of the federal government requesting any information concerning people who had bought a .22 rifle in the area. There was so much paperwork that arrived they didn't have enough manpower to sift through it all.

Lt. Duplantis and Capt. Comeaux decided to start going to all the local stores in St. Martin Parish and Iberia Parish trying to see if someone had sold any .22 rifles. After going to most all the stores in both parishes, they seemed to hit the jackpot.

Lt. Duplantis had gone to White's Auto Store in St. Martinville and found out the store had sold a .22 rifle to Elmo Patrick Sonnier. Lt. Duplantis knew Elmo and knew he was a convicted felon so how could he have bought a gun. He also remembered Elmo's description of what he looked like, was the same as reported by Alice a week before when she viewed the line-up and actually picked out Lt. Duplantis. He would try to locate where Elmo was living but only found out that he had moved out of St. Martin Parish.

The case seemed to grow stale. There wasn't much useful information coming in. The press, newspapers, TV stations and radio stations were still all reporting on the case, and this was causing everyone to live in fear. Parents wouldn't let their kids go anywhere without them, and the schools were on lock down.

There were hundreds of tips still coming in, some were so outlandish and others credible. Every tip that came in was investigated but wasn't getting them any closer to solving the case. There were several women who mentioned an old barn that looked like it was about to fall over. They reported they had been kidnapped, taken to this barn, and raped. None of them panned out. Oh, but one day, something came up, that would blast this case wide open.

Ron Alleman was a young deputy working in the patrol division. He was married, and his wife liked to have her hair done. One day, Ron's wife went to her hair stylist, and while there, she overheard another woman talking about a man who worked with her husband. The woman said her husband worked offshore on a barge and was telling her that a guy working for him, Eddie Sonnier, was acting strange. Every day, all day long, Eddie would sit to take a break and pull out a newspaper clipping of a photo of Loretta and start to cry. The lady's husband had once asked Eddie why he took the photo out and cried, and Eddie told him because the girl was so pretty, and it's a tragedy that she had to die like that.

When Deputy Alleman received this information, he immediately notified Capt. Comeaux and Lt. Duplantis. With all the time and effort put into trying to solve this case, Lt. Duplantis thought they might finally have the break they have been waiting on.

The next morning Lt. Duplantis informed everyone at the daily meeting about the information he had received and devised a plan to catch Eddie and bring him in for questioning.

During the meeting, Major Tyler had another good lead for the case. He reported the night before, a Major of the New Iberia Police Department had contacted him with a confidential informant who supposedly had information on the case.

Major Tyler reported he met at the New Iberia Police Department with the Major and the woman. The information he received was astounding. The woman told him that Elmo Patrick Sonnier's stepdaughter, Tabitha, was her babysitter. One night, Tabitha came to her home and told her that Elmo had admitted to his wife Helen Sonnier that he had murdered David and Loretta. Tabitha said her mom had told her what Elmo had said.

Later that evening, the confidential informant was getting ready to go out for the evening, and Tabitha was there to watch her baby when suddenly her front door flew open. It was Elmo Sonnier. He had just kicked her front door open. Elmo started threatening her and Tabitha, saying he would kill anyone who said anything to the police about what he had done to David and Loretta all the while waving a knife around. The confidential informant then grabbed a gun, pointed it at Elmo, and told him he better leave or she was going to blow him away. Elmo threatened her one more time and left out of the house.

Based on both of the stories and the information of Elmo buying a .22 rifle at White's Auto Store, Lt. Duplantis knew they were on to something and might, finally, be able to solve this case.

Chapter 10
Eddie, Here We Come

It was December 1, 1977, a beautiful day, cool outside, partly cloudy and it was the day Lt. Duplantis had been hoping for. What seemed like years, had only been 26 days since the investigation started. The Iberia Parish Sheriff's Office now had two possible suspects in Elmo Patrick Sonnier and Eddie James Sonnier case. It was time to go after them.

Knowing the two brothers, Lt. Duplantis advised Capt. Comeaux that Eddie would be the weak link. Eddie was younger, smaller, quiet and always followed Elmo. If Elmo told Eddie to jump, Eddie would ask how high. Eddie was not a leader, but he was a follower.

Chief Desormeaux received information that Eddie was working for F&R Construction Contractors at Houston Systems located at the Port of Iberia. The chief went to Houston Systems and spoke to the foreman, a guy named George. Chief Desormeaux told George he needed to speak to Eddie Sonnier. George took Chief Desormeaux to three different locations of the business, but they could not find Eddie.

Now worried Eddie might not be at the job site, Chief Desormeaux asked George if he can try calling Eddie on the intercom system. The business covered so much property. Eddie could be on the job, and they could have missed seeing him at one of the locations. George called Eddie over the intercom system, and sure enough, it worked. Eddie came strolling into the office. George pointed him out telling Chief Desormeaux that's him right there.

When Eddie entered the office, Chief Desormeax was standing there waiting for him. Seeing Chief Desormeaux, Eddie backed up a few steps and wanted to know what was going on. Chief Desormeaux told Eddie he needed to go with him to the courthouse. He had some questions to ask him.

Eddie wanted to change out of his work uniform, but Chief Desromeaux made him go the way he was dressed. The chief then verbally gave Eddie his Miranda rights, and Eddie said he understood them.

On the ride to the courthouse, Eddie wanted to know why he was being taken in for questioning. Chief Desormeaux told him that they wanted to talk to him about a car that was found abandoned in St. Martin Parish. Chief Desormeaux reminded Eddie, anything he said would be used against him in court. The chief did not want Eddie to know he was a suspect in David and Loretta's deaths so he didn't say anything about it.

Chief Desormeaux wanted Eddie to be comfortable, so he never handcuffed him and even let him ride in the front seat of his sheriff's department car. The ride to the courthouse was slow. Both Eddie and Chief Desormeaux were very tense. The Chief wanted so badly to unleash holy terror on Eddie, but he knew if he did anything he shouldn't do, Eddie might go free.

When they arrived at the courthouse, Chief Desormeaux brought Eddie straight to the 1st floor into Sheriff Wattingny's office where Sheriff Wattingny was sitting behind his desk. Det. Steve Davis and Major Sonny Tyler followed them into the office.

Once settled in the office they began to ask Eddie questions about the case in St. Martin Parish. Eddie was even asked if he would take a lie detector test, and he said he would, but he wanted one thing. Asked what was the one thing he wanted, Eddie told them he would take the lie detector test but wanted a lawyer with him. Chief Desormeaux told Eddie that would not be a problem.

Now was the time to drop the bomb on Eddie. Since Eddie never asked to have a lawyer present, he was fair game. Major Tyler then asked Eddie to tell him what he knew about the two kids murdered in the woods near a sugar cane field about a month ago. This startled Eddie. He froze, looked down at the glare from the freshly waxed floor, trying not to make eye contact with Major Tyler. Eddie then said he didn't know anything about murders.

Chief Desormeaux was again getting frustrated. Eddie wasn't giving them anything that would help in their investigation. In other words, Eddie wasn't giving it up. Then Eddie said something that shocked everyone in the room. He said he would tell them everything they wanted to know, but he would only tell it to one person. Sheriff Wattingny asked Eddie who is that one person? Eddie said he would only talk to Russell Duplantis.

Chapter 11
Eddie Says, "He Didn't Kill Them"

Chief Desormeaux walked out of the office and headed downstairs into the narrow stairs leading into the basement of the courthouse. The basement is where the detective bureau was located. Chief Desormeaux located Lt. Duplantis and told him Eddie wanted to talk but would only talk to him. Lt. Duplantis found this strange, but then again, he and Eddie have known each other for a long time.

Lt. Duplantis and Capt. Comeaux went upstairs and into the sheriff's office. Upon walking in, Eddie said, "Hey Russell."

Lt. Duplantis replied, "Hello."

Eddie continued, "They wanted me to tell them some stuff, but I won't talk to anybody unless you hear and tell me it's OK." Lt. Duplantis asked if Eddie had been read his rights, and Eddie said yea. Lt. Duplantis asked Eddie if he wanted to tell him about the murders.

Lt. Duplantis knew he had Eddie where he wanted him. He knew Eddie was weak and a follower. After all he had known Eddie since he was just a kid. Only a handful of people who worked for the sheriff's office knew of his past relationship with Eddie. You see, Eddie's mom was the sister of Margaret's father. Remember Margaret is Lt. Duplantis' ex-wife? Eddie and Margaret were cousins. Lt. Duplantis had actually been kin to Eddie by his marriage to Margaret. Little did he know back then that one day he would be investigating Eddie for a double homicide.

Lt. Duplantis hadn't seen Eddie since he divorced Margaret years ago. He had always known Eddie to be kind of slow when it came to reading and writing. He also remembered that Eddie was weak-minded and a follower. Meaning he was very easily influenced. He was never a person to get into trouble, but his brother Elmo was nothing but trouble.

Lt. Duplantis and Capt. Comeaux both sat across from Eddie who had been seated in a chair at a small table with a note pad and a pen. Everyone else in the office except Major exited the office. When they left, Eddie seemed to calm down.

Lt. Duplantis told Eddie to tell him what he had to say. Eddie told him he was involved in the deaths of the boy and the girl. Lt. Duplantis listened to Eddie's story and asked if he would give a written statement. Eddie agreed but reminded Lt. Duplantis he could not read and write too well. Capt. Comeaux volunteered to write the statement in Eddie's words. Lt. Duplantis asked Eddie if it was OK with him if Capt. Comeaux wrote his statement in Eddie's own words while he told about his involvement in the murders. Eddie said, "Yeah that would be good."

Lt. Duplantis asked Eddie if he had a photo of the girl, and Eddie pulled a photo of Loretta out of his wallet. When asked why he had a photo of Loretta, Eddie said he kind of knew her, she was from New Iberia. Lt. Duplantis asked how he knew her, and Eddie said, "We kinda gave her a ride one night." That's when he started opening up and telling them what happened that dreadful night.

Eddie said Elmo asked if he wanted to go rabbit hunting and he agreed. Elmo knew of a place not too far away in St. Martin Parish, and they went hunting. When they were driving up, they saw a white car. Elmo told him to stay in the car and hold the light.

Elmo went to the car, and he could see him talking to the kids. Elmo made them get out of the car and took their driver license. He then came to me and asked if Eddie would drive the white car, but he refused.

Elmo made the boy and girl get into the back seat, and he handcuffed them together. Eddie asked the boy what kind of car was this, and the boy said he didn't know but his dad worked for the sheriff and he got it from a sheriff's auction. Elmo drove, and Eddie sat in the front passenger side. Elmo drove around for a while and headed toward Olivier and went down a gravel road and turned on what looked like a board road, and there were some tanks. Elmo turned around and stopped the car, told Eddie to stay in the car, and he took the kids out. The boy said his name was David while they were driving.

Elmo took the boy and girl into the woods while Eddie stayed in the car. Elmo was just supposed to talk to them. It was taking a while, so Eddie went into the woods to try and find them. "I found them and saw the girl didn't have any clothes on, and David was handcuffed to a tree." Eddie told Elmo they were already in enough trouble. Elmo said he wasn't going back to the pen.

They all went back to the car, and Elmo told Eddie to get the big flashlight and make the kids lay on the ground. They laid down, and Eddie held the light while Elmo walked back to the car and got his .22 rifle. Elmo then shot one bullet into the back of the head of the girl and then one bullet on the back of the head of David.

David was laying on the left, and the girl on the right. We went back to the car, and Elmo went back to the kids and shot David two more times in the back of the head and then he shot the girl two more times in the back of the head.

They got back into David's car. They were scared so they headed back to Elmo's car in St. Martinville. When they got there, Elmo threw the car keys into the car, they got into Elmo's car, and left. Elmo took a right onto the black top road, and a-little-ways down, he tore up the driver license and threw them out of the window.

They went home, and Eddie couldn't sleep. He kept thinking about the girl. A few days later, Elmo told Eddie the cops are getting close so they took the guns and buried them. They are buried down Jefferson Island Rd.

Eddie told Lt. Duplantis there were several times he wanted to go to the police and turn himself in and tell them what they had done. He never went because he got scared.

Capt. Comeaux grabbed a statement form and pen and prepared to write the statement. What you are about to read now is Eddie's confession. The confession he gave to Lt. Duplantis while Capt. Comeaux was writing it down. The following came from the actual statement given by Eddie on December 1, 1977 and is written word for word:

On Nov. 4, 1977, my brother Patrick Sonnier and I was living on Jefferson Island Road. Patrick asked me if I felt like going hunting on are about 9:15 P.M. on Friday Nov. 4, 1977 We left in his car a 66 are 67 blue Dodge Dart. I asked Patrick where we were going, he said that we were not going far to see if we can pick up anything on side the road, like rabbits. Patrick was driving the car and he was headed towards St. Martinville passing on the road where the drive inn is in New Iberia. We went through St. Martinville and headed towards Cypress Island. Patrick told me why don't we check into the side roads, to see if they had any lovers parked. Patrick drove down a road that leads off the main road and we saw a white car parked. Patrick told me to stay in the car and shine the light. Patrick got out and he did not have any weapons with him. He went to the car and asked to see there driver's license. They gave Patrick their driver's license and said that they wouldn't give him any trouble. Patrick came and asked me if I could drive the white car. I told Patrick I wasn't going to drive it. Patrick told me he would drive it. He told the boy and girl to get into the car and I got into the car also. Patrick said that he would leave car there. Patrick then hand cuffed the boy and girl together and Patrick drove the car. I asked the boy what kind of car was it. He told me but I don't remember, however the boy told me the car had been bought at a Sheriff's auction and this was once a deputy sheriff car. We rode around St. Martinville around while the boy and girl seated together on the back seat handcuffed. Patrick still driving the car headed toward Olivier and headed down a gravel road. It looked like there was a board road. We went to the end where the tanks are and turned around. We came back a little piece and stopped. Patrick Sonnier, my brother, told me to stay with the car and made the girl and David LeBlanc get out. David LeBlanc had told me his name while we had been riding. Patrick took David and the girl in the woods. Patrick was supposing to just take them into the woods and just talk to them. However, I thought it was taking long. I walked towards to where they were in the woods, I saw that the girl did not have any clothing on. I saw David was in woods handcuffed to a tree. I told Patrick that we were already in enough trouble. Patrick told me that he wasn't going back to the penitentiary. He made the girl dress and had them come to where the car was. Patrick told me to get the flash light in the car, a silver colored flashlight that holds two or three batteries. Patrick told me to shine the light on David and the girl then he told them to lie face down. Patrick had gone to get the rifle out of the trunk of car. Both the girl and David was lying down Patrick shot the girl first once then shot David. He shot David once and I told him he was crazy. Patrick told me that he was not going back to the pen. That's when he went back and David twice and then the girl twice. The girl was lying down on the right side and David was on the left after shooting both David and the white female Patrick threw the rifle into the car. Patrick was driving we got scared and took off back to where his car was parked in St. Martinville. After David car was parked Patrick threw the keys of David's car into the woods next to David's car. Leaving the road where David's car was Patrick took a right on the black top about a half-mile down Patrick tore the driver's license that he had taken from David and the girl. They were thrown out the window as he had pulled the car a little bit off the road. We then came back home. I don't remember the time we got back home. We had picked up David and the girl on this road between 10 and 10:30 PM Patrick wore gloves all the time. Patrick wipe the handles on the door when he parked David's car. A couple of days later Patrick told me they were getting close and had some evidence and that something should be done with the gun. Patrick and I went and buried the gun. The gun is a .22 automatic and was bought from Paul Vincent who lives in the *project the handcuffs are usually left in the trunk of his car and I Don't know if he has them still. On several occasion I felt like calling the sheriff's office but I just couldn't make up my mind.*

All this statement have been given of my own free will. I have been given my rights and understand them. I have waved my rights.

My brother full name is Elmo Patrick Sonnier.

The statement was dated December 1, 1977 with time 3:55 p.m. and signed by Eddie Sonnier, Capt. Horace Comeaux, and Lt. Russell Duplantis.

Eddie signed the statement, and Lt. Duplantis asked him about Elmo. Eddie said Elmo works for Jo De Equipment Rental in New Iberia. He drives trucks for them and was in Galveston today. He would be back later tonight. Eddie then gave Lt. Duplantis a very strong warning, "If you go after Elmo, be ready, because he always carries a .38 gun with him, and he will use it. Elmo doesn't want to go back to Angola."

Chapter 12
We Found the Gun

Lt. Duplantis asked Eddie if he would show him where the gun was buried, and Eddie agreed. Eddie was placed in handcuffs and lead out of the courthouse and placed into the back seat of Lt. Duplantis' department car. Capt. Comeaux rode on the front passenger side, while Lt. Duplantis drove the car.

Eddie told Lt. Duplantis to go down Jefferson Island Rd. toward Delcambre. When they arrived near the oil tanks, the same location Missy had reported she had been raped, Eddie told Lt. Duplantis to turn left. It was an open field right across the other side of Jefferson Island Rd. from the oil tanks. They exited the vehicle and Eddie started pointing to where he thought the gun was buried.

The open field was desolate. The grass was dead in several large areas, and there was an old railroad track crossing over the property from east to west. They searched and searched the area trying to locate where the gun was buried. Eddie finally decided to tell them Elmo had marked the area by putting sticks in the ground.

After searching for what seemed like hours, they found the location where the sticks were sticking up from the ground. Not having a shovel, Lt. Duplantis, Capt. Comeaux, and Eddie all started digging with their hands. Lt. Duplantis felt something and pulled it out of the hole. It was a green plastic material with something inside. Lt. Duplantis asked Eddie if this was the gun, and Eddie told him yes. Lt. Duplantis asked Eddie why the gun was buried in the green plastic material, and Eddie told him, "So we could come back and get the gun and go do it again."

Lt. Duplantis then drove them back to the courthouse. Capt. Comeaux tagged the green plastic material and prepared it to be taken to the Acadiana Crime Lab the next day.

The next day when the lab technicians opened the green plastic material, it contained two .22 cal. rifles which had been taken apart and placed in the green plastic. Capt. Comeaux said he only knew of one gun.

A warrant was prepared and signed by Judge Robert Johnson charging Eddie James Sonnier with LA. R. S. 14:30 First Degree Murder. Eddie was placed under arrest and then taken to the Iberia Parish Jail located on the 4th floor of the courthouse and booked into the jail. He would spend many days in the jail.

While incarcerated in the Iberia Parish Jail, Eddie reported that he was getting some strange letters. Letters that someone knew what he did and was going to kill him. The letters were later proven to be written by Eddie to himself. Why did he do this? No one really knows.

Now with Eddie out of the way, it was time to focus on Elmo Patrick Sonnier. Elmo was a very big guy, mean guy, tough guy, who would be harder to take into custody than his younger brother Eddie.

Chapter 13
The Stakeout

Lt. Duplantis and Capt. Comeaux went to Jo De Equipment Rental and spoke to Harry, who was the foreman at Jo De Equipment Rental. Harry told them Elmo Patrick Sonnier was in Galveston and due to be back in New Iberia later that night.

Harry told the detectives that Elmo would arrive near the east side gate and would get out of the truck to unlock the gate, drive the truck inside the gate and park the truck. Then he will leave the truck there and go home. Harry gave Capt. Comeaux a key to the Jo De Rental Equipment gate.

Sheriff Wattingny called a meeting at the courthouse to formulate a plan on catching Elmo when he gets back into town. Everyone conferred back and forth on the safety of the mission and how to catch Elmo without anyone getting hurt. The plan had to go down like clockwork.

Sheriff Wattingny decided he and Chief Desormeaux would drive to Lafayette and watch Interstate 10 for the truck Elmo was driving. Once they see the truck, they would follow it back to New Iberia, and when it gets close, the sheriff would get on the radio and say code word "Green lantern." Sheriff Wattingny told them he watched a new television program by the same name and liked it. He then ordered one deputy to go to Elmo's residence to keep an eye on the family and not let anyone answer the phone or make any calls. He didn't want anyone being able to tip off Elmo they were waiting for him.

Lt. Duplantis, Major Tyler, Detective Davis, Deputy Musemeche, Deputy Ron Alleman, Detective Ray Boudreaux and Capt. Comeaux would all stakeout Jo De Equipment Rental in separate locations, making sure they would not be seen. Deputy Musemeche was designated as the sniper and given permission if Elmo pulls out his .38 caliber gun, to shoot him. All other officers hid behind pipe in the yard of the business and behind other buildings near the business.

It took about two hours but eventually Sheriff Wattingny called over the radio, "Green lantern." It was time to take Elmo into custody. As with any operation of this kind, everyone was nervous. If anything went wrong, someone could die or suffer a bad injury.

Within a few minutes, the truck could be heard coming down the road. It turned onto Darcey St. and was coming straight toward them. It was the moment of no return. If Elmo would see one of the officers, he might try to run over them with the big flatbed truck he was driving. If he made it to the gate and saw one of the officers, he might pull his .38 caliber gun from under the driver seat and start shooting. Most officers would prefer for Elmo to just lay down on the ground and give up. Guess what? None of this happened.

The truck drove up to the gate and stopped. Elmo opened his door and then closed it and started reaching under the driver seat where he kept his gun. The officers had what is called the pucker factor on high alert. The pucker factor is being nervous, scared, brave, stupid and stressed all rolled into one. Most cops know the feeling well.

When a law enforcement officer is involved in a high-risk take down such as this, the adrenaline starts flowing and you get excited but in a scary way. No one wants to die, but you're putting yourself in a position where you could be killed. Everything happens so fast; decisions have to be made in a fraction of a second and it better be the right decision. These are the moments that a cop lives for. He relishes, and he hates these situations all at the same time.

If you ever talk to former police officer about his job in law enforcement, he would say he missed the job. Why? Because of the old saying *"it's in the blood."* The true meaning to "it's in the blood" for a police officer is the adrenaline rush he gets from pressure situations like the one that is just about to happen.

Elmo looked out the truck window and slowly opened the door. He stepped out of the truck and turned back as if he was reaching for the gun. Suddenly, he turned and walked toward the gate. He put his hands in his pockets while the officers watched and pulled out the keys to unlock the gate.

Lt. Duplantis ran toward Elmo, but it seemed as if everything was moving in slow motion. Major Tyler appeared out of nowhere telling Elmo, "Freeze! You're under arrest." Detectives, Davis and Ray Boudreaux along with Deputy Alleman grabbed Elmo and pushed him against the fence and handcuffed him.

Lt. Duplantis looked at Elmo, and there was something dripping from his pants. The officers had scared Elmo, "*the big bad serial rapist/murderer*," so bad that he peed in his pants. Lt. Duplantis wanted to laugh but suddenly heard his name. When he looked up, it was Elmo saying, "Russell, Russell, is that you?"

Lt. Duplantis replied, "Yes Elmo, it's me."

Before another word could be said, Major Tyler gave Elmo his Miranda rights. He said it word for word as if he was reading it off of a Miranda rights card. It was perfect words for the officers after the adrenaline rush each of them just experienced. They all knew Elmo had killed before and would kill again before going back to the pen. Everyone was happy the plan went off without a hitch. No one was hurt, and not one round was fired from a gun.

Elmo was then transported to the courthouse and taken up into Sheriff Wattingny's office on the 1st floor. During the ride and while sitting in Sheriff Wattingny's office, Elmo complained about the handcuffs being too tight. Lt. Duplantis thought to himself, *Elmo you acting like a big baby.* That Elmo never once worried about how tight he put the handcuffs on all those young boys. Forcing them to watch as he raped their girlfriends.

Lt. Duplantis wanted to tell Elmo how much of a piece of shit he was. If there ever was a time in his life he wanted to hurt someone, it was now, and it was Elmo he wanted to hurt.

All the horrible things Elmo had done, all the people he hurt was running through Lt. Duplantis' mind.

Elmo was in the sheriff's office with Sheriff Wattingny, Chief Desormeaux and Major Tyler. Elmo was again given his Miranda rights. Elmo said he knew his rights and didn't need a lawyer. They began to ask him questions, but he wasn't answering any of them. Chief Desormeaux was again getting frustrated and then heard the same words Eddie had spoken earlier. Elmo said, "I won't talk to anyone but Russell."

Chapter 14
Elmo Says, "I Killed Them"

Lt. Duplantis and Capt. Comeaux entered Sheriff Wattingny's Office. When Lt. Duplantis entered the office, Elmo said, "Hey Russell, I need to talk to you." Lt. Duplantis asked Elmo if he had been given rights, and Elmo said yeah.

"Okay, now let's hear what you have to say."
Elmo then looked up at Lt. Duplantis and said, "Eddie talked, didn't he?"

Lt. Duplantis said, "Yes he did. He already told us everything. He was very cooperative with us."
Elmo shook his head left to right saying, "One day I'm gonna get a hold of that boy and they are gonna bring him home to Gladys in a pine box."

Elmo gave us a blow by blow of the case as close as to what we knew of the case. We figured he probably left some things out, but he did admit to kidnapping the kids and bringing them to a country road off of Crochet Road on a little headland and executed them.

Elmo said that night he and Eddie went rabbit hunting on Seiber Road, and when they were leaving, Eddie saw a white car with a young couple in the back seat. Eddie said he was going to have some fun scaring the kids. This was all supposed to be a big joke.

Eddie went to the car with a flashlight, hollered this is the police while flashing a badge, saying what are y'all doing on private property. The kids were taken out of the car, and they took their driver license. Eddie told them he would have to talk to the property owners and see if they wanted to file charges on the kids for trespassing. They made the kids get into the back seat of the boy's car, and Elmo drove the car. They drove for a while, and he knew of a location in Iberia Parish. He drove to Crochet Road and then onto a sugar cane field headland near some oil tanks.

Lt. Duplantis asked Elmo why did he have to kill the two kids. Elmo replied that he had noticed the back doors to the boy's car did not have any door handles on inside the car. He asked the boy why there were no handles, and the boy told him something that would scare Elmo and make him commit murder.

Back in the 1970s, when law enforcement would buy a new car for patrol, they would remove the rear door inside handles to keep suspects from escaping from the car. There were no child safety locks on cars like they have today.

Elmo explained that the boy told him his dad worked for the sheriff out of St. Martin Parish and the sheriff helped his dad get the car from a sheriff's auction. He said he panicked because he and Eddie had kidnapped the kids out of St. Martin Parish. At that point, he knew that he would be going back to Angola if it was out, he had kidnapped the kid of a sheriff's deputy in St. Martin Parish. He could not deal with going back to Angola. As soon as the boy told him his dad worked for the sheriff, the boy signed his and the girl's death warrants.

Elmo said they got out of the car. He stayed with the boy while Eddie took the girl into the woods to talk to her. It had been a while so he went and checked on them and saw Eddie having sex with her. He told them to get dressed and come to the car. He was upset because he thought he had talked the boy into not saying anything if they let them go.

When they arrived back at the car, Elmo took Eddie to the back of the car and told him he was stupid, and he wasn't going back to Angola for accessory to rape.

"Now you know what we gotta do?" Eddie said.

"No what do we have to do?"

"Now we gotta **kill** them." We had them lay down on the ground and with the boy on the left and the girl on the right. Elmo held the flashlight while Eddie fired one round at the girl and missed. Elmo grabbed the gun and fired one round into the back of the girl's head and then one round into the back of the boy's head. He then fired two more rounds into the back of both the girl and boy's heads to make sure they were dead.

After killing the boy and girl they ran back to the boy's car, got in and drove back to Seiber Road to get his car. He noticed he had a flat tire on his car and knew all he had was a little jack in his car and didn't feel like fighting with it. He checked the boy's car and found a bigger jack. He used that jack to change his tire and placed the jack in the trunk of his car because he was going to give it to his wife. She didn't have a jack for her car.

Elmo then wiped down the door handles of the boy's car and they drove off leaving the girl's purse and other belongings in the car. A few days later they went and buried the guns.

Lt. Duplantis told Elmo they had already found the guns, why did they bury the guns in the green plastic. Elmo's reply was, after the dust settled, we were going to go back and get them and do this again.

Elmo confessed to being at the murder scene with Eddie, and he is the one who shot them kids, not Eddie. After giving a full confession Elmo was asked to write a written statement of what had taken place. Elmo said he wasn't too good at writing. Capt. Comeaux wrote Elmo's statement for him in Elmo's own words.

You are about to read the statement given by Elmo Patrick Sonnier. This is written word for word from Elmo's actual statement that he wrote on December 1, 1977:

On November 4, 1977 my brother and I went rabbit hunting in the back of St. Martinville. We left our house on or about 9PM. We had gone in my little blue Dodge Dart. Eddie and I came out towards our car from the woods. Eddie Sonnier my brother got out of the woods first then came back and tell me that there was a car in the front of mine. We sat in the weeds for a little while. While we were sitting down in the weeds my brother said that he would go and see if he could scare them, but the mosquitos were eating us up and we wanted to get out of the woods. My brother Eddie went out to the car with his rifle. He walked to the car and hit on the glass and the girl started screaming. My brother opened the front door and told them to shut up. That's when I came out and meet them. I asked Eddie what was going on That's when he started preaching about parking on private property to the boy and girl in the car. I then asked them what they were doing at that time of morning this was between the hours of 1:30 AM and 2 AM we both got into their car, I got behind the wheel my brother Eddie was on the passenger side and the boy and girl both white were made to get in the back seat of the car. Before getting into the white couple's car which the boy and girl was in when I placed my rifle into the trunk of my car. Eddie asked me for my handcuffs I had them with me. I told Eddie yes that they were in a brief case in the trunk of my car. I got the handcuffs and gave them to Eddie. While I was driving the car, Eddie put the handcuffs on the white male and female on the back. They had to crawl over the seat to get into the back seat when Eddie had made them get in the back. We left the area off the Seiber Road and drove to St. John Refinery and came around St. Martinville the back way towards New Iberia. We went on the Loreauville Road and turned right on a gravel road. I had gone down that road several times and knew where the road was at. I also knew that they had a road that led off this road but I had never gone down that road. I turned down this road and went to the end where the tanks are turned around and stopped on the side of the road. My brother and I got out we walked to the back of the car. We were talking Eddie I trying to decide how to let them kids go without them telling on us. I took the boy who told me his name was David, but I didn't ask him his last name. When the white girl had gotten out of the car on this road in the back of Olivier Eddie took the handcuffs off the girl and left them on the boy. I walked to the left of where the bodies were found and Eddie walked into the woods with the girl. I talked to David about not saying that the gun was pointed at them. I believed that I had him convinced into not

64

saying anything and even took the handcuffs off and had them in my hand. I asked David if he would stay by the car and I would go get his girlfriend and my brother. I walked in the direction which they had left. I walked towards them and they both had their clothing off and Eddie was on top of the white female. Eddie was having intercourse with the girl, this was on a headland between the woods and sugar cane. I walked up and asked Eddie what he thought he was doing. He Eddie answered what the hell you think I'm doing. I told them to both get up and put their clothes on. I called Eddie to the side and I told him he had done a stupid thing. I had the boy convinced why he didn't try and convince her instead of pulling a stupid stunt I then told him, I guess you know what we will have to do. Eddie ask me what we have to do. I told him that we couldn't let these people go after this, because I would be charged with accessory to rape. I asked him what he intended to do about it. I told him that he had a gun in his hand to use it. Eddie had brought the rifle with him when he brought the white female into the woods. The white female, Eddie and I walked out of the wooded area to meet David by the car. Eddie told me that he couldn't shoot too good. We both made David and the white female lay down on the ground. The female was on the right and the male on the left. Eddie took one shot and missed; I was holding the flashlight. I then took the rifle a .22 automatic and gave Eddie the flashlight. I then shot both David and the white female who was lying face down on the ground and I know I didn't miss. When my brother fired the girl started crying but David never said anything and never offered resistance. After I shot David and the white female, I gave the gun back to Eddie. We got into David car and drove back on the road off Seiber Road. When we got there my car had a flat. I took the jack out of David's car to raise my car because I didn't have a jack. After using the jack, I put it into the trunk of my car and we took off. I left the car keys to David car in the ash tray and mixed them up with the cigarettes. I wore gloves all the time and when I brought the car back, I wipe the door handles. I did not mess with any of their belongings or had their driver's licenses with *me, from there we went home. I must go back before I shot David and the white female that when Eddie the white female and I came out of the woods, the white female told David that she had sexual intercourse with Eddie, naming Eddie's name. David got red in the face and you could see he was angry and would of fought if he thought he could of won. However, I did not say anything. The following night my brother Eddie and I went and bury two rifles. They were wrapped in green plastic bags with three boxes of .22 shells. The bag was also taped with black electric tape. Of the two rifles in the bag one of them was not used. The rifle that was used has marks name on it and the day I gave it to him. The oldest barrel goes to the stock with Marks name on it. The original owner was Paul Vincent who sold it to this boy from whom I purchased it from. I can't recall his name but Paul Vincent would know. I bought the other rifle in the green plastic bag from Paul Vincent for $30.00. The rifle was used in the killing of these two people I paid $15.00 for it.*

The statement was dated 12-1-77 with the time 11:40 p.m. and signed by Elmo Patrick Sonnier, Lt. Russell Duplantis and Capt. Horace Comeaux.

After giving his statement, Elmo looked at Lt. Duplantis and told him he had a feeling all day long that today was his last day of freedom. He had thought about it all the way back from Houston. He thought about how he was going to fight his way out of being caught.

A warrant was written up charging Elmo Patrick Sonnier with LA. R. S. 14:30 First Degree Murder and signed by Judge Robert Johnson. Elmo was then booked into the Iberia Parish Jail.

Chapter 15
Search Warrant Equals Evidence

A search warrant was drawn up and signed by Judge Robert Johnson to search Elmo's home located on Jefferson Island Rd., all vehicles and any other buildings on the property.

While conducting the search of Helen Sonnier's (Elmo's wife) car, deputies found the jack that was taken from David's car. It was located in the trunk. Elmo had admitted in his statement that he kept David's car jack.

David's father would later identify the jack as the jack he bought and put into the car David was driving. He had bought it for David's sister.

When the search of the home was conducted, a pair of handcuffs were located in Elmo's bedroom. They were not a fake pair, not a toy, they were the real thing.

A search of Elmo's blue Dodge Dart would reveal another very important piece of evidence. Throughout the entire investigation the Iberia Parish Sheriff's Office and the St. Martin Parish Sheriff's Office thought the suspects were using some type of security badge. They would use the badge to identify themselves as law enforcement to get the kids to comply with them.

What they were going to find in the car would shock everyone involved in the investigation. And once again, it would hit Lt. Duplantis like a ton of bricks.

While searching Elmo's car, deputies found a badge. An Iberia Parish Sheriff's Office patrolman's badge. Yes, you read that correctly. Elmo had an actual law enforcement badge. How did they get this badge? Did they steal it from someone? No one knew until Lt. Duplantis remembered something about his past.

Lt. Duplantis had been married to Margaret for about 12 years. They were still together when Lt. Duplantis was promoted to Detectives and was given a detective's badge. A few years later he and Margaret split up, and when he was moving out of the house, he couldn't find his old patrolman's badge. He never found it.

The badge Elmo and Eddie were using to kidnap these kids and rape all these young girls was Lt. Duplantis' old patrolman's badge.

Years later, Lt. Duplantis visited Elmo in Angola, asked Elmo how he was able to get the badge, and Elmo told him the story. When Margaret had lost her home to the bank, she needed help moving out. Elmo and Eddie helped her move. Eddie had gone into one of the bedrooms and removed the drawers from a dresser so he could carry the dresser out. In one of the drawers he found the badge, stuck it into his pocket and kept it. They used it during their crimes.

Lt. Duplantis remembered Margaret had moved out of the house about 1½ years earlier. If Elmo and Eddie had started using the badge right after, then how many more victims are there? How many girls have been raped that they didn't know about? Did Elmo and Eddie kill others' kids that they didn't know about?

Many years later, Lt. Duplantis was approached and asked if he wanted the badge. Lt. Duplantis didn't want any part of the badge and turned down the offer.

While still searching the area, Lt. Duplantis noticed the old barn that looked like it was about to fall over. He remembered all the women who reported being kidnapped and taken to an old barn saying it looked like it was about to fall over.

Lt. Duplantis and Capt. Comeaux found some old boards and braced the barn so it wouldn't fall on top of them while they searched it. Inside the barn they found an article of clothing that matched what one female said, she was wearing the night she had been raped.

The ballistics report for the two rifles and the .22 cal. ammo came back. It reported the rifle Elmo said was used in killing David and Loretta matched the bullets removed from their heads during the autopsy. The .22 cal. ammo that was found with the guns in the green plastic material also matched the rounds that were fired from the rifle.

Lt. Duplantis still had several questions that were unanswered. He went to the jail and asked Elmo if he would be willing to go to the scene at Crochet Road and explain to him the locations and events that took place when David and Loretta were murdered and Elmo agreed to go.

Lt. Duplantis and Capt. Comeaux transported Elmo to the crime scene at Corchet Road. Elmo then proceeded to show them where Eddie had sex with Loretta, which was a clearing in the woods near the headland on side of the sugar cane field. He pointed out where the car was parked the night of the murders which was near the trash pile and showed Lt. Duplantis where David and Loretta were forced to lay face down on the ground on top of the trash pile when he shot them. From what Lt. Duplantis knew from his investigation of the scene, everything matched up perfectly. The only way Elmo could have known about the crime scene was that he would have had to have been there when the crimes were committed.

Elmo would eventually give a recorded statement and another verbal statement of what happen the night of November 4, 1977 into the early morning hours of November 5, 1977. His story for the most part stayed the same with only a few discrepancies.

Chapter 16
Grand Jury

Assistant District Attorney, Dracos Burke, worked diligently preparing himself to take this case before the grand jury. Mr. Burke called every officer involved in the case and set up meetings with them and went over the case. Lt. Duplantis and Capt. Comeaux kept Mr. Burke up to date on the case as it unfolded.

Mr. Burke knew that he could bring Elmo and Eddie to trial for all of the rapes they committed. He did not want to muddle up the case and get a jury all mixed up. He was going for the death penalty and with so many rape cases that it could pose as a real problem.

When Lt. Duplantis went in to talk to him, Mr. Burke told him he wasn't going to try the rape cases and explained why. If he tried the rapes cases with the murders this could cause the jury to get all mixed up so he would only try the murder cases. If for some reason Elmo and Eddie are found not guilty in the murder cases, his ace in the hole was the rape cases. He could always come back and try Elmo and Eddie for the rapes.

The grand jury convened in December 1977 just two weeks after Elmo and Eddie were arrested for the murders of David and Loretta. The grand jury would come back with a true bill. Both Elmo and Eddie were indicted on first-degree murder charges.

Sheriff Wattingny moved both Elmo and Eddie to other local jails in nearby parishes because it was too dangerous for them in Iberia Parish. The sheriff was worried someone would try to kill the brothers. Vigilante justice was not going to take place under his watch.

Chapter 17
The Trials

On April 12, 1978, Elmo's trial would begin. Judge C. Thomas Bienvenue presided over the case. It would last for three days.

The following explains how the new death penalty law works:

The United States Supreme Court halted executions in the U.S. from 1969 to 1977. During the summer of 1976 the U.S. Supreme allowed for the death penalty to return, but with new rules. The first rule was there had to be two separate phases of the trial for the accused. The first phase was to prosecute the suspect and see if he or she would be convicted. The second phase would begin right after the first one. This phase was to determine if the suspect after being convicted, met one of the five aggravated circumstances during the crime to qualify for the death penalty.

The five aggravated circumstances listed by the U.S. Supreme Court are 1) Aggravated Burglary, 2) Armed Robbery, 3) Aggravated Kidnapping, 4) An especially heinous atrocious crime or cruel manner, 5) Risk of death or great bodily harm to more than one person. This meant that for the death penalty to be given one of these had to have taken place during the murder.

Mr. Burke knew he had to make sure of every little detail. You see, this was the very first case to test the new death penalty laws that were established by the US Supreme Court.

If Mr. Burke failed to win this, we probably would never have had the death penalty again in the United States.

Jury selection for Elmo Patrick Sonnier's trial began on April 10, 1978. After picking the jury, the trial started. When Elmo walked into the courtroom, he was smiling. It seemed like the jury was intimidated my Elmo.

The trial ended on April 14, 1978. Mr. Burke called over 20 witnesses to the stand. Eddie even testified at the trial saying Elmo was the shooter. Elmo testified in his own trial, and he said he took part in the commission of the crime, but Eddie was the shooter.

Years later before he was executed, Elmo admitted to Lt. Duplantis that he and Eddie had devised a plan. Eddie would point the finger at Elmo as the shooter and Elmo would in turn point the finger at Eddie as the shooter. Their thought was, if both blamed the other, the jury would not know who to believe and they both could only get life in prison. I guess their trials didn't go according to their plan.

The jury deliberated for only one hour and 20 minutes and came back finding Elmo guilty of first-degree murder. Now the second phase would begin to see if Elmo's case met any of the aggravated circumstances for a death penalty sentence.

Mr. Burke, during the second phase, was able to prove not just one but all five aggravated circumstances that took place during the commission of this crime. Only **ONE** was needed, but this case had all **FIVE**. On April 16, 1978, the jury deliberated and voted 12-0 in favor of the death penalty. Elmo was formally sentenced to death on April 25, 1978.

Jury selection started on September 11, 1978 for Eddie's trial. The trial started on September 12, 1978 and ended on September 13, 1978. Eddie testified in his trial again saying, Elmo was the shooter, and Elmo testified in Eddie's trial again saying Eddie was the shooter.

In the first phase, Eddie was found guilty of first-degree murder. The second phase was completed, and the jury found Eddie guilty saying again all five aggravated circumstances took place in the commission of this crime. Eddie, like his brother Elmo, received the death penalty.

Eddie would appeal his case and get a new trial because according to the US Supreme Court, if two people were involved in a death penalty case, only the person, the one who actually committed the murder could be sentenced to death. Eddie had proven in his first trial that he took part in the murders of David and Loretta, but he only held the flashlight while Elmo shot and killed them. During this trial, Eddie was again found guilty of first-degree murder, but this time he was sentenced to life in prison.

Chapter 18
Eddie's Second Trial

Eddie Sonnier appealed his case to the Louisiana Circuit Court of Appeals and won a new trail. The appeal was based on the new United States Supreme Court Law stating if two or more people are involved in a capital murder case, and it warrants the death penalty, just because someone participated in the crime doesn't mean they get the death penalty. The person would have had to actually help perform the murders. What Eddie's lawyer's focused on was that Eddie held the flashlight while Elmo killed Loretta and David.

In their first trials, Eddie claimed Elmo was the shooter and Elmo claimed Eddie was the shooter. Their reasons for blaming each other as the shooter was two-fold. The first is: blaming each other, which means they wouldn't implicate themselves in the trials as being the shooter. The second is: if they blamed each other, who would the jury believe?

A few weeks before Eddie Sonnier's second trial was to begin, Mr. Burke received a letter. The letter didn't come through the mail; it was hand delivered. The letter came from Rufus George, a short, thin, dark-complexioned man. He was the kind of guy that liked to laugh all the time. Rufus was an inmate and was doing six months in the Iberia Parish Jail for public intoxication. When sober, Rufus was everybody's best friend. When he drank, he wanted to fight; didn't win not one fight, but he wanted to fight.

Mr. Burke, curious about the letter, opened it and to his surprise, it was from Rufus, who was an inmate in the Iberia Parish Jail. Rufus wanted to testify of what Elmo told him while they were in the same jail cell together. This is the letter:

Mr. Dracos Burker
Assistant District Attorney
Iberia Parish, Louisiana 70560
Dear Mr. Burke,

What I'm about to tell you must be kept strictly confidential until the time my testimony is required in behalf of the state for reasons of security. If Elmo Sonnier finds out before my testimony is given, he will kill me. The information I'm going to give must be kept strictly confidential between yourself and Mr. Kowles Tucker only, do not even mention it to any member of the Sheriff's Department or Elmo Sonnier will find out.

Elmo and Eddie Sonnier both told me and my cell mate that he "(Elmo)" killed those two teenagers.

They also told me and my cell mate about their plan. Eddie said if he got off the death sentence as he did, he was going to say he really killed those kids.

This was the state could not give him the death sentence again. Also, he said he was going to say Elmo his brother didn't do nothing so he could get off the death sentence too. This new trial and false confession is all a plan of Elmo and Eddie's to get Elmo off.

I, sending you a clipping of which I read. The whl thing is a lie for Elmo to get a new trial as they said you bunch of suckers would probably buy it.

Elmo is always talking about killing somebody in here or killing somebody when he gets out. Elmo said he would kill anybody who tried to mess him up so keep it quiet. My cell mate and myself will testify for the state about this.

I'll tell you everything if you call me down. Please do not draw any attention or Elmo will kill me.

Rufus George

Mr. Burke, starting to feel overwhelmed prosecuting both Elmo and Eddie and having to file motions against all the appeals, did not really want to have to retry Eddie. But because of Eddie's appeal to the Louisiana Circuit court, he would have to return to the old drawing board. Mr. Burke, having already tried Elmo and Eddie, knew the cases like they were yesterday's news. He would again go after Eddie for the death penalty. He would have Rufus and his cellmate testify in the trial.

Mr. Burke was once again successful in trying Eddie Sonnier. He had the same witnesses as he had for the 1st trial. He attacked the case the same way he had the first trial. Being the man he was, Mr. Burke went after Eddie with everything he had.

Eddie Sonnier was again found guilty of first-degree murder. There was a difference this time around. The jury felt Elmo, not Eddie, was the shooter. Elmo was the one responsible for taking Loretta and David's lives.

The jury knew Eddie did play his part in the crimes but did not feel he pulled the trigger. The second phase of the trial, the sentencing phase started, and when the jury deliberated, they came back with life in prison. Eddie Sonnier was no longer on death row. He would spend the rest of his life in prison.

Was this a win for Eddie? Would he rather spend the rest of his life in prison, or would he rather go ahead and die on the electric chair? When Eddie was granted a new trial, he wasn't trying to get life in prison. He wanted to go free. Be out in the world enjoying life. But when the jury came back with the guilty verdict, Eddie just sank in his chair. He was going back to prison, and this time it would be forever.

Eddie, having been given life in prison, figured he would do whatever he had to do to help save Elmo's life. After testifying in his own trials and Elmo's first trial saying Elmo was the shooter, he now changed his tune. From the day he received life in prison until his death in 2013, Eddie would now say he was the shooter and Elmo just held the flashlight. Eddie knew he could never receive the death penalty again so it didn't really matter now if he changed his story. He felt he had to help Elmo.

The plan was a good idea, but it never panned out. Elmo was never granted a second trial. Eddie would never be able to testify in court for Elmo saying he was the shooter and that Elmo only held the flashlight.

Eddie, not being able to testify in another trial for Elmo, did do what he could. Eddie would write a letter to Louisiana Governor, Edwin Edwards, claiming Elmo was not the shooter. Eddie told Governor Edwards in his letter that he is the person who killed Loretta and David. The letter was given to Governor Edwards while Elmo was filing his last appeals just before his execution. The letter didn't work.

Chapter 19
A Nun Comes to Town

I want to make it clear that you, the reader, understand that a nun representing the Catholic Church, Sister Helen Prejean, author of, *Dead Man Walking,* never mentioned in her book or in the movie that she came to New Iberia to visit Elmo Sonnier in the Iberia Parish Jail. She wrote that she was his pen pal and met him in Angola in 1982. She would also write the first time she ever touched Elmo was when they were walking him to the electric chair for execution. After reading this chapter, you will see that she wasn't so forthcoming in her book. Why would she not write that she used to visit Elmo in the Iberia Parish Jail? Keep reading and you will find out. I'm sure if you were in her shoes, you wouldn't write about it either.

There is no record available to show the exact date, but sometime in 1978, a nun by the name of Sister Helen Prejean arrived in New Iberia. She was in town to see Elmo because she was his spiritual advisor through the Catholic Church. She had been writing him letters for a while and now wanted to visit him in person in the Iberia Parish Jail. Based on the information obtained for this book, it is very well possible Sister Helen had been visiting Elmo at Angola first and when he was sent to New Iberia for his appeals, she started visiting him there.

Sheriff Wattingny allowed her to visit with Elmo in the Iberia Parish Jail. They would meet alone just the two of them in Elmo's jail cell. Eddie's Sonnier's cell was right next to Elmo's cell. Little did Sister Helen know but, because of her and Elmo's behavior, her visits alone with Elmo would come to an end.

A big investigation would be conducted by the United States Department of Justice in New Iberia. The investigation would be centered on Sister Helen and Lt. Duplantis.

Sister Helen would visit with Elmo on a semi-regular basis. It was not an everyday thing. When she would come to visit Elmo, she always wanted to visit him alone. Just the two of them. Why? Lt. Duplantis knows the real answer.

Lt. Duplantis received information from jail trustees that Elmo and Sister Helen Prejean were doing things in Elmo's jail cell that were not allowed to happen in jail. Lt. Duplantis reported this to Capt. Comeaux, and Capt. Comeaux told him to try and catch them in the act. The next time Sister Helen came to New Iberia to visit Elmo, she was again allowed to visit him alone in his jail cell. But they wouldn't be alone for long.

Lt. Duplantis waited about 20 minutes into their visit, then went to the jail and quietly walked up to Elmo's cell. What Lt. Duplantis saw taking place caused him to immediately remove Sister Helen from the cell. And to think in her own book, Sister Helen wrote the first time she ever touched Elmo was when she placed her hand on his shoulder while he was walking to the electric chair.

Lt. Duplantis told Sister Helen she had to go with him. He took her to Sheriff Wattingny's Office. Lt. Duplantis told Sheriff Wattingny what he saw, and Sheriff Wattingny advised Sister Helen she was no longer allowed in his jail to visit with Elmo. This would set off a firestorm.

Either Sister Helen or someone she knew pulled some strings through the Catholic Church and had someone contact the United States Department of Justice. They reported to the Department of Justice that Sheriff Wattingny was violating Elmo's civil rights by not allowing her to visit with him alone as his spiritual advisor. The US Department of Justice came into New Iberia and conducted an investigation to see if in fact, Elmo's rights were being violated. All because Lt.

Duplantis caught Sister Helen and Elmo in an act prohibited in the jail.

The Department of Justice's investigation could not prove Lt. Duplantis or Sister Helen's side of the story of what took place that day in Elmo's jail cell. The Department of Justice informed Sheriff Wattingny that even though they weren't able to prove what happened in Elmo's jail cell, he still had to allow Elmo to have his spiritual advisor visit with him. This did not sit well with Sheriff Wattingny and did not mean Sister Helen could still visit with Elmo alone. Sheriff Wattingny said, he had no problem allowing Sister Helen to visit with Elmo, but from this day forward, every time she came to visit Elmo, there he would have a deputy stationed at the door of the jail cell. They would not be left alone again.

Why did Sister Helen fail to mention this in her book? Is there something she doesn't want everyone to know? Does she have something to hide? Yes, she does. She probably felt she would not get the sympathy and support from the public if they knew the real story.

Lt. Duplantis told me exactly what he caught Sister Helen doing with Elmo that day in his jail cell, but I cannot write it in this book. You, as the reader, will have to come to your own conclusions. It shouldn't be hard to figure it out.

After Elmo's execution, Lt. Duplantis was asked if he had heard Elmo's last words to Sister Helen. They were, "I love you," and her last words to him were "I love you too." His reply was no he hadn't heard that, but if they did say those words to each other, he knew why. Because he knew of the kind of relationship they had all along.

In a later chapter, I will be writing about Lt. Duplantis' last visit with Elmo at the Angola State Penitentiary. Elmo requested to see Lt. Duplantis one last time before his execution. Lt. Duplantis always had some unanswered questions, and during this visit, Elmo gave him most all the answers. This included admitting to Lt. Duplantis the kind of relationship he and Sister Helen had together. Let's say it's not a relationship as spiritual adviser; it was much, much more.

Chapter 20
Elmo Files Appeals Before Execution

Elmo and his attorneys would begin the long process of appealing his case all the way up to the Louisiana Supreme Court. The court upheld Elmo's conviction saying his case met all the requirements set forth by the US Supreme Court for the death penalty. A date was then set for Elmo's execution. Unfortunately, the date kept getting set back as Elmo and his attorneys kept filing appeal after appeal.

Elmo was represented by Allen McElroy for his trial. Later, when Elmo was filing all of his final appeals before his execution date, he was represented by Attorney William 'Bill' Quigley.

Mr. Quigley was recruited by Sister Helen Prejean to represent and file the appeals for Elmo to try and stop his execution. An article in the *Daily Iberian Newspaper* dated Sunday, April 8, 1984, titled, 'Sonnier: Burke reveals hectic last-play moves,' mentions a nun who was Elmo Sonnier's chaplain, asked Mr. William Quigley to take on Elmo's case for one last run.

Here is the article in the *Daily Iberian* I just mentioned:

The Daily Iberian
Sonnier: Burke Reveals Hectic Last-Play Moves

The Man who prosecuted Elmo Sonnier said the drive to save him from the electric chair was rather like the New Orleans Saints trying desperately to march 90 yards to a game-saving touchdown after the two-minute warning.

If the difference hangs tough, it usually won't work—and Assistant District Attorney Dracos Burke of New Iberia was all over the field on this one.

"We went through the entire state and federal court systems in 12 hours, Burke said. "That's extraordinary.""

"I think if we had fallen behind at any point, any one of those courts could have said, "Hey, we just don't have what we need to decide this," and issued a stay."

Anti-death penalty forces wanted a new trail, or at least another delay. Burke wanted Sonnier eliminated. He won a conviction at Sonnier's District Court trial in New Iberia in 1977 for killing two teenagers during a lover-lane orgy of rape and murder and he wanted the jury verdict carried out.

THERE WAS NO *claim of innocence. The plea contended only that there were imperfections in the trial preceding, and that although Elmo took part in the crime his brother Eddie was the actual killer.*

The final paper chase cranked up last Sunday, four days before the scheduled execution, when a nun who was Sonnier's chaplain got New Orleans Lawyer William Quigley to take on the case for one last run.

Burke said he discovered that Quigley was into the legal equivalent of the two-minute drill in professional football, in which a team runs a series of pre-determined plays without wasting time for a huddle.

Quigley had delivered appeals papers to the state District Court, to the state Supreme Court in New Orleans, and the U.S. District Court in Opelousas at the same time, and was poised to go to the federal courts of appeal Burke said.

"**WHAT HE DID** was file the plea in this court and deliver appeals to clerks in the other courts to hold until he telephones with instructions to file," said Burke. "We, in effect, had to do the same thing."

In a crash operation, Burke drafted a 35-page legal brief rebutting points raised on the appeal and had them hand delivered by couriers.

One after another, three courts rejected the plea and the scramble moved to the federal appeals courts.

"By the time it reached the 5th U.S. Circuit Court of Appeals I had run out of couriers so I telephoned the state attorney general's office in New Orleans, dictated my brief and they typed it up, signed my name to it and hand-carried it to the 5th," he said.

"That night the three-judge panel of the 5th circuit got us all on the phone in a conference call to ask questions," said Burke. "They didn't give us a decision, they just hung up. But then they said no and it went to the U.S. Supreme Court."

Burke used Telex at Rep. Billy Tauzin's office here to transmit his written arguments to Washington and telephoned the Supreme Court clerks to make sure "that each justice had our side of the case."

BURKE SCOFFED AT the defense plea that Eddie Sonnier, not Elmo, was the triggerman in the murder of Loretta Bourque, 18, and her fiancé David LeBlanc, 16, of New Iberia.

"You have to be extremely naive to believe that," he said. "I understand that the nun believes it, but she takes it on faith."

Burke said Elmo Sonnier, after his arrest, took officers to the scene of the kidnapping, leading them to exactly the spot where the bodies had been found a month earlier.

"He re-enacted the crime," he said.

Police then moved Elmo to jail in nearby Lafayette for the fear there might be an attempt to lynch him.

"On the way, he wasn't interrogated but he was bitching out loud," Burke recalled. "He said if Eddie had not gone up to the car (where the teenagers were spooning) I never would have had to kill those people and when I get in Angola I am going to send him back to mama with a tag on his toe."

"Both men, arrested separately and kept separate, made a confession, and in all reasonable respects it dovetailed," Burke said.

Eddie Sonnier also drew the death penalty in his separate trial in New Iberia but the Supreme Court reduced it to life in prison on the claim that Elmo was the actual killer.

THE APPEAL FEATURED a letter written by Eddie Sonnier to Gov. Edwin Edwards proclaiming himself the guilty one and volunteering for another trial in an effort to save his brother.

"You can't try a man a second time for the same crime, so he knows that legally that can't be done," said Burke.

"They tried to pull this once before," he said, referring to the trial of Elmo's death penalty, ordered by the state Supreme Court due to an error at the trial.

"Eddie took the stand at Elmo's second trail and lied about it. But what does perjury mean to a man facing two life sentences for murder?"

Chapter 21
The Execution

Elmo's appeals ran out. It was time for his execution. Lt. Duplantis and Capt. Comeaux were asked if they wanted to attend the execution, but both turned down the invitation. They had to endure the investigation, the trials and the appeals. They knew Elmo was guilty of murdering Loretta and David. Seeing him die would do nothing for them. They knew if they attended the execution, it would not bring Loretta and David back to their families.

On April 5, 1984, Elmo Patrick Sonnier was executed in the electric chair at the Louisiana (Angola) State Penitentiary. Sister Helen Prejean was there with Elmo till the end. Right before being executed as Sister Helen explained, Elmo looks up at her and says, "I love you," and she looks back at him and says, "I love you too."

After the execution, Sister Helen took the responsibility of giving Elmo a proper burial. It might have been a proper burial for most people, but Elmo was not most people. He was a convicted murderer who admitted to being a serial rapist.

Bishop Stanley Joseph Ott presided over the service, and Elmo was then laid to rest in Roselawn Memorial Park Cemetery. This cemetery is usually reserved for Catholic bishops and nuns. Why would anyone want to bury a cold-hearted murderer/serial rapist amongst Catholic bishops and nuns? I guess only Sister Helen would have the answer.

Eddie James Sonnier would die in Angola State Penitentiary on December 19, 2013. He was buried in the Angola State Penitentiary cemetery. He served 36 years in prison before he died. He didn't get all the fanfare like his brother Elmo by Sister Helen Prejean. He wasn't buried in Roselawn Memorial Cemetery. There was no Catholic bishop to perform his funeral services. Why? Because Sister Helen believed Eddie, the younger, smaller, weaker of the two brothers, was in charge the night of the murders and he was the one who pulled the trigger of the .22 cal. rifle that killed Loretta and David.

Why did Sister Helen believe Eddie was the shooter? Because that's what Elmo told her? A man who had on three occasions admitted to law enforcement officers that he, not his brother, had killed Loretta and David. The man who was older, bigger, stronger, had a criminal record, had served time in Angola, and was known to boss his younger brother around. Did Elmo follow his younger brother Eddie's orders on the night the two innocent teens were brutally murdered?

If you believe Sister Helen Prejean, you would think Eddie, the younger brother, smaller, weaker, brother who had never been locked up in Angola would have been in charge. Elmo is the brother who said he will do whatever it takes to never go back to Angola. So which brother was the one who pulled the trigger killing David and Loretta? All the evidence proves Elmo was the shooter.

Remember the confidential informant and Elmo's stepdaughter Tabitha? Remember Tabitha told the informant, Elmo had confessed to his wife Helen Sonnier, which is Tabitha's mother, that he killed the two kids? Didn't the informant say Elmo went to her house waving a knife threatening to kill her and Tabitha if they ratted him out?

Elmo had confessed that he drove David's car to Crochet Road the night the kids were murdered. Are we supposed to believe Elmo, when at any time, he could have gotten out of the car and not listened to Eddie? At any time, Elmo could have turned the David's car around and went back to his own car and left? There never was anything said in all the trials that Eddie threatened or used physical force to make Elmo do anything the night of the murders. Would it have been believable with Eddie being much smaller, and much younger than his older brother Elmo, that Eddie was in charge?

87

Why would an innocent man confess to killing two kids to only later say his brother did it? He confessed to the killings after he knew Eddie had been arrested and cooperated with the officers and gave them the whole story. When Elmo was arrested, he and Eddie didn't get to see each other and come up with a matching story.

During my many years of law enforcement, I have interviewed many victims, witnesses and suspects. I have learned when someone lies, the next time you interview them, they cannot remember what they said the previous interview because it was a lie. But when it's the truth, people can remember usually very easily. For Elmo to confess that he was the one who killed Loretta and David, confess on three separate occasions, wouldn't it seem that he was telling the truth? When Elmo changed his story and started lying, that is when his story was no longer believable.

Eddie Sonnier denied he killed Loretta and David from the start. The first day he was brought in for questioning he said Elmo killed the kids. The only time his story changed and said he was the brother who killed the teenagers was after his sentence had been reduced from the death penalty to life in prison. Why? Because Eddie knew he could not be tried a second time for the same crime and he had already been found guilty and sentenced to life in prison. He could not be tried again. He could not be given the death penalty. He only changed his story to try and save Elmo's life.

Where were the handcuffs found? In Elmo's bedroom. Who did the handcuffs belong to? Elmo. Who had the handcuffs with him the night of the murders? Elmo. Whose idea was it to go rabbit hunting that night? Elmo. Who claimed ownership of both rifles? Elmo. Where was the jack to David's car found? In Elmo's wife's car. Where was the badge located? In Elmo's car. For a man who wasn't in charge, how did he come to have everything from the crime in his possession? Remember, Elmo is the brother who never showed any remorse.

Which of the brothers would take the photo of Loretta out of his wallet and show remorse by crying? Eddie. Who said he thought about turning himself in but couldn't get himself to do it? Eddie.

This list could go on and on, but I think you get the picture. Elmo and Sister Helen were accusing Eddie as being the shooter when everything pointed to Elmo. Eddie was now saying he was the shooter because he could not get the death penalty and was trying to save Elmo's life.

For all the questions that had been left unanswered, Lt. Duplantis was about to get all the answers.

Chapter 22
One Last Visit

Elmo's execution date was getting close. Other than his spiritual advisor Sister Helen, Elmo was told he could have one visitor to come visit him before his execution. The visitor that Elmo chose was none other than Lt. Russell Duplantis. Why would he want to talk to Lt. Duplantis again? Maybe you will understand at the end of this chapter.

Lt. Duplantis was no longer working for the Iberia Parish Sheriff's Office when he was notified Elmo wanted to talk to him one last time before he would be executed. Lt. Duplantis didn't want to go but remembered he had so many unanswered questions. If he went and spoke to Elmo, with Elmo only having a few days before his execution, maybe just maybe he will give Lt. Duplantis all the answers to the questions that still bothered him. On the other hand, if Elmo wanted to be spiteful, he wouldn't answer the questions and Lt. Duplantis would go the rest of his life not having the questions answered.

Lt. Duplantis spoke to Capt. Comeaux, and he decided he would like to go with him. They contacted Sheriff Romo Romero and told him they would be taking the trip to see Elmo and they requested using one of his department cars. Sheriff Romo told them no. He was not letting them use a department car to go to Angola.

Lt. Duplantis spoke to former sheriff, 'Sheriff Gerald Wattingny.' Sheriff Wattingny loaned Lt. Duplantis and Capt. Comeaux one if his cars from his security business and called the warden at Angola to set up the visit with Elmo.

Lt. Duplantis and Capt. Comeaux were supposed to be at Angola around 9:30 a.m. They wanted to be there early so they arrived at 8:00 a.m. When they arrived at the gate, the guards advised them they were expecting them.

Lt. Duplantis and Capt. Comeaux were searched for weapons and any type of recording device. Those items were not allowed in the prison. They were escorted to a building which Lt. Duplantis explained he would later find out it was the death row building.

Both men were taken into a room and told where they were going to be seated for the visit. There were two guards that would be present at all times. Before being seated they were told they could not touch Elmo, and he wasn't to touch them.

After waiting about 15 to 20 minutes, Lt. Duplantis heard the most God-awful sound he had ever heard. It sounded like chains and metal dragging the floor. They didn't know what was going on then suddenly Elmo appeared at the door. He had chains covering his body from his shoulders to his waist on down to his feet. Lt. Duplantis had never seen anyone with so many chains on before.

Elmo was escorted into the room and sat at a small table on a chair across from them. He thanked them for coming saying, he didn't think they were going to show up. The prison employees never told Elmo they were coming to visit him. Elmo looked at Lt. Duplantis and said, "They told me I could have one visitor, and Russell, I chose you."

Elmo said he knew they were going to execute him real soon and he didn't want Lt. Duplantis feeling guilty and have to live with what they are going to do to him. He didn't want it on Lt. Duplantis' conscience. Lt. Duplantis told Elmo, "I really don't have a problem, and I'm not bothered by it."

Elmo said, "You know they are going to execute me and I just didn't want it to bother you." It was as if Elmo was trying to get into Lt. Duplantis' head.

Lt. Duplantis leaned forward in his chair looking straight into Elmo's eyes and told him, "I'll sleep just like a baby after you're executed. I have no sympathy for you." Elmo looked back at Lt. Duplantis with a big smirk on his face.

Elmo then told them several things they didn't know about the rapes, and he even went into great detail about how he and Eddie did it. Lt. Duplantis asked him how many couples they had kidnapped and raped, and Elmo said he stopped counting after he hit about 15. There were many, many more after that. It had been going on forever.

Lt. Duplantis recreated the crime scene, and Elmo didn't skip a beat. He remembered everything like it was yesterday. He talked about it with no remorse whatsoever.

Elmo asked Lt. Duplantis if he remembered that nun Helen. Lt. Duplantis shook his head yes and said, "I do." Elmo said she fell in love with him. Because he knew this, he had bull-shitted her. His exact words were 'bull-shitted her.' He went on to say she believed he was in love with her, and she even wanted him to marry her. She asked him to marry her if she could get him a life sentence instead of death row. Then he laughed and said, "Can you imagine me marrying a nun?" while shaking his head side to side.

Lt. Duplantis asked Elmo who shot David and Loretta. Elmo said he was the one who shot David and Eddie is the one who shot Loretta. They laid them down on the ground, and the boy David asked if he could hold the girl's hand, and he said yes you can hold her hand. She reached her hand toward David's, and he held her hand. That's when we shot them.

Elmo said, "It was the nun."

Lt. Duplantis asked, "What do you mean it was the nun?"

Elmo said, "It was the nun, who came up with the idea about Eddie changing his story, saying he shot them kids instead of Elmo. Her thought was Eddie was weak and slow in the mind and would be easy to get him to say he shot those kids. If Eddie would say he shot them, I might get a new trial and life in prison instead of the death penalty." That's how bad she wanted to marry him.

Elmo told Lt. Duplantis that David was a man, a real man. Not once did he ever beg for his own life. He begged for the girl's life, even offering himself to save her life. David could have fought with us and being a big boy might have had a chance. He could have run off into the woods and gotten away because they had un-cuffed him, but he never ran. All that boy cared about was being there with his girlfriend. He knew if he fought them or if he ran away, they would shoot the girl because they had the guns pointed at her, not him. He kept saying, "Kill me and let her go. She won't tell anyone." Elmo told David he couldn't do that and that's when they told them to lay down on the ground.

Lt. Duplantis asked Elmo if he ever had any remorse for what he had done, and Elmo told him, "No, never, none whatsoever." He never dreamed about it, not one time, and it never bothered him. "Eddie was bothered about it, especially about the girl and had problems sleeping afterwards. But as for me, no, never ever bothered me."

Lt. Duplantis remembered finding the guns buried in green plastic. He asked Elmo why did he bury the guns in the green plastic, and Elmo's response was exactly what he thought he would hear. Elmo said he buried them so the cops wouldn't find them, and when everything died down, he was going to dig them up and do this all over again.

Chapter 23
The Movie

The character Matthew Poncelet was played by Sean Penn in the movie, 'Dead Man Walking.' He was a combination of Elmo Sonnier and Robert Lee Willie. This was done in the movie, 'Dead Man Walking' but not in her book.

There are a few similarities in the two cases. Elmo Sonnier and his brother Eddie Sonnier raped and murdered Loretta Bourque and David LeBlanc. Robert Lee Willie and his friend Joseph Vaccaro raped and murdered Faith Hathaway and kidnapped and raped Denise Morris. Elmo received the death penalty, and yet Sister Helen claims it was Eddie that committed the murders. Robert received the death penalty, and yet Sister Helen thinks Joseph committed the murder.

Det. Mike Vanardo wrote a book titled, *Dead Man Walking: The Forgotten Victims*, which is about his investigation of the rape and murder of Faith Hathaway. His investigation led him to arrest Robert Lee Willie and Joseph Vaccaro. Robert Lee Willie would get the death penalty, and Joseph Vaccaro would get life in prison. This is the same thing that happened to Elmo and Eddie Sonnier.

PBS interviewed Det. Mike Vanardo, Faith Hathaway's mother Elizabeth Harvey, Debbie Morris, and Sister Helen Prejean. While reading the transcripts of interviews, some interesting information came into focus.

Det. Mike Vanardo makes a comment that struck a chord. He said that another detective told him that Sister Helen is after the Nobel Peace Prize because she's certainly not trying to give anyone spiritual advice to try and save their souls.

Remember Lt. Duplantis saying he caught Sister Helen and Elmo doing inappropriate things in Elmo's jail cell? Funny she never once mentioned in her book that she used to visit Elmo Sonnier when he was in the Iberia Parish Jail.

Another issue came up in the interview. If Sister Helen is really trying to save those on death row, then why does she charge people for her autograph? Could it all be about the money?

Det. Mike Vanardo explains how he has tried to rationalize the death penalty. He doesn't take pride in people being executed and was having a tough time dealing with it. His spiritual adviser told him to read Romans, Chapter 13. Since reading this chapter, he has been able to move forward. He knows not every person who commits murder deserves the death penalty but the ones like Robert Lee Willie do.

The interview with Elizabeth Hathaway is heart breaking. She talks about finding out her daughter Faith had been murdered and how she was in denial. Her whole life was turned upside down.

Elizabeth and her husband Vernon Harvey have made it their life's work promoting the death penalty. Each time there is a scheduled execution at Angola, they are there to show their support for the victim's families.

Debbie Morris, during her interview, tells how she was kidnapped and raped by Robert Lee Willie and Joseph Vaccaro. She says Robert was the leader; the man in charge, and she explains why she thought he was the man in charge. She was held captive by Robert, and Joseph for over 30 hours.

When PBS interviewed Sister Helen, she actually proved that she is ignorant to the horrific things people can and will do. While she admits Robert Lee Willie was involved in the death of Faith Hathaway, it almost seems as if it didn't matter. She thinks Robert Lee Willie only held Faith's head while Joseph Vaccaro decapitated her. She thinks Joseph was in charge even though another victim, Debbis Morris, says Robert was in charge. Basically, Sister Helen believed Robert Lee Willie when he said Joseph Vaccaro actually murdered Faith Hathaway the same way she believed Elmo Patrick

Sonnier when he said it was his brother, not himself, that murdered Loretta Bourque and David LeBlanc.

I think I would have a tendency to believe the other victim Debbie. After all, she was the one who was there and experienced what the monster, that was Robert Lee Willie, was capable of.

Sister Helen's actions with both Elmo and Robert looks a lot like she has a pattern. It seems like almost every time she is sent to give spiritual advice to someone on death row, she thinks they were involved in the crime but not the person who actually committed the murder. I'll say it again. Sister Helen believes the persons on death row for murder did not commit the murders. They were murders committed by their accomplice. After all the trials and appeals, she believes a death row inmate who has admitted to committing multiple rapes when he said he didn't commit murder.

Sister Helen actually explains her own ignorance in the interview. She explains that Robert Lee Willie wanted so bad to take a lie detector test, to prove to his mom, that he didn't kill Faith Hathaway. The test was set up.

Guess what? Robert Lee Willie fail the lie detector test. What does Sister Helen do? She says that because of the way Robert Lee Willie felt, how badly he wanted to prove to his mother that he did not commit the murder; he must have been stressed when he took the lie detector test. The stress caused him to fail the test.

Detective Vanardo mentioned during his interview that the Bible is the Bible. It says what is says and doesn't change. He goes on to say that Sister Helen changes the Bible and its teachings to fit her own needs. She uses certain parts when they are convenient.

Sister Helen, from what I've read, has been the spiritual adviser for many people on death row. What I haven't read is that any of these people changed their life and gave themselves to God with her as their spiritual adviser. Sister Helen was the spiritual adviser for the Boston Marathon Bomber. She came out and said, the bomber who is Muslim had converted to Christianity while she counselled him so he shouldn't get the death penalty. Think about this for a moment. A Muslim terrorist who bombed Americans at the Boston Marathon has converted from Islam to Christianity.

From the actions of Sister Helen Prejean, is she really trying to stop the death penalty? Could it be that she is trying to say the people that she counsels that are on death row are innocent? She is the only person who can actually answer these questions, but with some of her actions, it makes it very easy to what her motives could be.

Chapter 24
Attempting to Right a Wrong

Sister Helen Prejean's book, *Dead Man Walking* has several inconsistencies, half-truths and outright lies. She claims to have only been Elmo's spiritual adviser yet the words in her own book tell a different story. Could this have been a book based on a love affair? Did Sister Helen Prejean fall in love with Elmo Sonnier? A man who admitted he was a serial rapist that she also knew was a murderer. A man who admitted he killed two innocent teens and later changed his story blaming his own bother for the murders.

I will attempt to point out parts of Sister Helen's book, *Dead Man Walking* as being a lie, misleading or just never happened. This is all based on Lt. Duplantis' story and from the actual case file provided by the Louisiana's 16th Judicial District Attorney's Office.

Two Big Lies:

Sister Helen writes: "the pathologist testified the small circumference of the wounds indicated that the shots had been fired at close range with the muzzle of the weapon against the skin of both Loretta and David." The coroner, Dr. Joseph Musso never testified the barrel of the gun was against Loretta or David's skin. In fact, he testified the gun shots were from close range maybe four feet. Sister Helen also wrote Pat (as she always called Elmo Patrick Sonnier) said, he was about 8 feet maybe more from Loretta and David when they were shot. She also fails to mention the FACT that Eddie Sonnier and Elmo Patrick Sonnier both confessed they were about 4 feet away when the shots were fired.

Sister Helen writes: David's father Lloyd LeBlanc told her, "he would have been content with imprisonment for Patrick Sonnier." There is no way to prove Mr. LeBlanc did or didn't say this but the next line in her book states, "He says that when he arrived with sheriff's deputies there in the cane field to identify his son, he had knelt by his boy – laying down there with his two little eyes sticking out like bullets – and prayed the Our father," and said, "Whoever did this, I forgive them." To me, this is biggest lie in the entire book *Dead Man Walking*, which contains so many. How can Sister Helen claim Mr. LeBlanc identified his son at the crime scene? David and Loretta were first identified by using their class rings to get possible names of the victims, and the families were then contacted to go to the Iberia Parish Morgue and identify the bodies. Chief Jim Desormeaux had testified for the grand jury and at both Eddie and Elmo's trials, stating how the bodies were first identified by their class rings and then later by family members at the morgue. Why would Sister Helen, a Catholic nun, lie in such a way? What good did this do for her? Did it make her feel better? No. The real reason she did this was to make Elmo Patrick Sonnier look human instead of the MONSTER he really was.

Was Sister Helen in Love with Elmo Patrick Sonnier?

The following is the page number and what Sister Helen had to say in her book *Dead Man Walking*.

Sister Helen writes, "the Angola Prison Chaplin would later try to bar her and other women as spiritual advisers to death row inmates."
Sister Helen writes: "the first time she saw Elmo Patrick Sonnier he had a handsome face." (She never said this about Robert Lee Willie.)
After Elmo was executed his personal effects were delivered to her instead of his family.

Sister Helen writes: "a glimmer from a recent dream flashes: Pat Sonnier in a red-and-black plaid shirt, alive and smiling and sitting in my living room. I'll have to tell Pat about the dream. Maybe he'll see it as a good omen."

Sister Helen writes: "she fainted and had to be taken by ambulance to the prison hospital. Before she is taken away, she tells Capt. Rabelais, Please tell Pat what happened, he will be worried."

Sister Helen writes: "He (Pat) looks up at me and says, 'Thanks for loving me,' but I feel guilty that so much love has been lavished on me."

Sister Helen writes, when she put her hand on Pat while he was walking to his execution: "He is tall. I can barely reach. It is the first time I ever touched him." I guess she forgot she used to visit with him in the Iberia Parish Jail and was alone with him in his cell. And of course, she would never mention Lt. Duplantis catching her and Elmo in the cell together doing something that is not allowed to be done inside a jail.

Sister Helen writes: "she kisses him before she was led away to the viewing room to watch Elmo's execution." Then she writes: "Elmo looked up at her and told her, 'I love you,' and she told him, 'I love you too.'"

Sister Helen writes: "when she was leaving the prison after the execution a reporter asked her if she was in love with Elmo."

Sister Helen writes: "pretty bad things being said about me at the prison, that I was emotionally involved with Pat Sonnier and that I had caused a lot of trouble with the fainting episode."

Sister Helen writes about Eddie Sonnier: "He has taken to calling me Sis. It fits. I know I'm family to him."

Sister Helen writes: "her plea at Pat's Pardon Board Hearing was easy for Pat but not for Robert." I guess her feelings for Pat made it easy to say something good about him and not so easy for Robert.

Guards didn't like death penalty?

Sister Helen writes: "a trustee (whom she doesn't name) told her that he had never saw anyone with more remorse than Elmo Patrick Sonnier." I have to wonder if she was talking about the same Elmo Patrick Sonnier that Lt. Duplantis knew for so many years and eventually became a serial rapist/murderer, Lt. Duplantis came to know of Elmo.

Sister Helen writes: "One of the guards had said to me this morning, as I came through the visitor center, that the Angola 'grapevine' had it that the 'wrong brother was getting the chair.' She came up with another unnamed guard." Again, no name of the guard.

Sister Helen writes: "she was talking to a guard sitting inside the door. The guard told her, 'I don't particularly want to be here, you know what I mean, doing this, being part of this, but it's my job. I got a wife and kids to support'." So again, another unknown guard is against Elmo's execution.

Sister Helen writes: "Shortly before the execution in Louisiana of a convicted murderer, Tim Baldwin, on September 10, 1984, a guard in the death house whispered to him, 'you gotta understand Tim, this is nothing personal'." What is the name of the guard? She didn't give one.

Sister Helen writes: "unnamed guard pulls her aside saying, I don't want to be a part of this." Did this guard have a name?

Sister Helen speaks of a conversation she had with Major Kendall Coody, the head of the Department of Corrections, before he died of a heart attack. She wrote: "What a spot to be in, Major Coody, the warden and most of the guards around here. He can't persuade himself that he's doing his job." So again, she mentions unnamed guards, unnamed warden and Major Coody who is deceased.

Are You, The Reader, Starting to See a Pattern Here?

Sister Helen writes all these guards basically told her they were against the death penalty, but none of them seem to have a name.

Chapter 25
Let's Write a Book

Lt. Duplantis and Det. Sgt. Scott Hotard, the author of this book, met each other when Lt. Duplantis moved back to New Iberia from Georgia. Lt. Duplantis started working for the Iberia Parish Sheriff's Office Work Release Center. At the time, Det. Hotard was the lieutenant in charge of the Criminal Investigation Division. They didn't really talk much back then but would say hello in passing.

In June 2013, Sheriff Louis Ackal wanted to start a new program for the elderly. He chose Det. Hotard to start up and run the Crimes against the Elderly Division. Lt. Duplantis was working in the same office building as Det. Hotard.

Lt. Duplantis and Det. Hotard learned that they had a lot in common. They both have basically followed the same career path. Both worked patrol, crime scene, detectives and supervisor of detectives. Both have worked and solved many homicide cases. Having basically the same background, Lt. Duplantis knew Det. Hotard understood him and what he felt about this case. It was for this reason only that Lt. Duplantis and Det. Hotard decided to write this book. Lt. Duplantis knew Det. Hotard would be able to give the story through the eyes of a detective. A homicide detective who knows the pressures and feelings that come with each case.

Lt. Duplantis told Det. Hotard he investigated the Elmo Sonnier and Eddie Sonnier case. After several conversations, they decided, together, that it was time people heard Lt. Duplantis' story. Sister Helen Prejean gave her story in her book *Dead Man Walking* and the Bourque family told their story in their book *Dead Family Walking*. Now Lt. Duplantis was going to give his side of the story. The actual detective that investigated this case. The one who knows the untruths told by Sister Helen Prejean in her book *Dead Man Walking*.

Det. Hotard conducted several recorded interviews with Lt. Duplantis. Det. Hotard and Lt. Duplantis took several trips to the scenes where all the crimes took place. The location where Elmo was arrested, the home Elmo and Eddie lived in when they committed these horrible crimes in 1977, and locations of many rapes. While at each location, even after 40 years, Lt. Duplantis was able to show Det. Hotard the exact locations of the crime scenes and where everything took place.

Det. Hotard contacted the 16th Judicial District Attorney Bo Duhe about viewing the case file for this case. Mr. Duhe was kind enough to allow Det. Hotard access to the original case file to help write this book. The photos you see in this book are photos that were taken from the actual case file along with photos from the actual crime scenes 40 years after later.

Closing

Lt. Russell Duplantis carried his feelings about his investigation into the murders of Loretta Bourque and David LeBlanc for over 40 years. Now, with his story out there, hopefully, Lt. Russell Duplantis can finally put this case, a case that has haunted for so long, behind him. The truth is now being told.